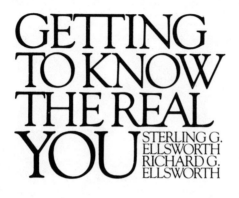

GETTING TO KNOW THE REAL YOU

STERLING G.
ELLSWORTH
RICHARD G.
ELLSWORTH

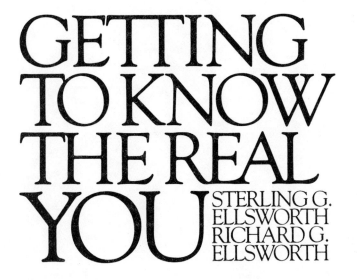

GETTING TO KNOW THE REAL YOU

STERLING G. ELLSWORTH
RICHARD G. ELLSWORTH

Deseret Book Company
Salt Lake City, Utah
1980

Contents

1

Remember Who You Are

Now the Lord had shown unto me, Abraham, the intelligences that were organized before the world was; and among all these there were many of the noble and great ones;

And God saw these souls that they were good, and he stood in the midst of them, and he said: These I will make my rulers; for he stood among those that were spirits, and he saw that they were good. . . .

And there stood one among them that was like unto God, and he said unto those who were with him: We will go down, for there is space there, and we will take of these materials, and we will make an earth whereon these may dwell;

And we will prove them herewith, to see if they will do all things whatsoever the Lord their God shall command them;

And they who keep their first estate shall be added upon; and they who keep not their first estate shall not have glory in the same kingdom with those who keep their first estate; and they who keep their second estate shall have glory added upon their heads for ever and ever. (Abraham 3:22-26.)

As a young man I often heard the admonition "Remember who you are."

Most often these words would be said to me by my father

just as I was leaving to go out for the evening, free from parental watch or guidance—out for fun, and adventure and escape from the humdrum of life. My father would look at me and say soberly, "Remember who you are"—and I would think, "Why does he always say that? I know who I am." Mentally, I would recall my name and address, and go blithely on my way.

But now that I am older and more experienced, I see that my father meant much more than I had supposed.

There are more dimensions to our being than are apparent to us with our presently available physical senses. We come to this life, as William Wordsworth poetically sensed it, "trailing clouds of glory . . . from God, who is our home." We come as volunteers, eager to succeed, eager to experience, eager to learn what earth life has to teach us. We are eager to prove ourselves able in the midst of pleasure and pain. And although our memory of our pre-earth life is taken from us that we may act and be acted upon, fairly, without restriction, yet our *identity* as powerful, successful, and ethereally beautiful spirit sons and daughters of divine parents is not changed at all.

This identity always remains. It is ours, and it is always there, always available, whether we are aware of it or not. It is our spirit self. It is the "real me," the "deep down inside soul" that so many people are struggling to uncover and to know. It is the sacred individual essence that is particularly our own anywhere and everywhere no matter who or what we are in our mortality. It is the foundation upon which our lives here upon earth were meant to be built.

It was this, then, that my father meant when he advised me from the depths of his earth-life experience, "Remember who you are." He meant that I should, in a sense, continue to keep my first estate, maintaining a clear view of my most basic identity. He knew that if I would remember always *who* I was, and also *who* everyone around me was, my life and actions would be much different than they might otherwise be. He knew from his own experience that true happiness in this life and out of it is based upon keeping that point of view and acting in accord with it. And he knew that my growing, my being "added upon" would be increased or decreased as I lined up my earth life with spiritual reality.

But most of us soon learn that earth life is extremely earth centered. It is very easy to lose our spiritual way. Often we are even taught by our parents and our loved ones that we have little or no spiritual identity, that we have only this earthly life. Society presses upon us, and the mortal competition for success and status distorts our perspectives, cluttering us with habits and desires that are foreign and muffling to our real selves. Our thought and our expression become blunt and fuzzy. We become insensitive. We hardly even know what we are thinking or saying, let alone what others are saying to us.

A while ago, a couple who had marital problems came to my office. They sat on opposite ends of my couch, trying to tell me what was happening in their relationship and how it was happening. Harry was trying to tell his side of the story, and Blanche was trying to tell hers, both at the same time because neither knew how to listen to the other. I began to notice a pattern. Every time Harry would say something Blanche would make a fight out of it. "No, it wasn't *four* at all. It was *three*." "No. That's not right." "You are wrong." And so on and on. She continually interrupted everything he said.

Finally I said, "Blanche, why don't you let Harry finish his sentences?"

She interrupted me before I had finished the question. "I *do* let him finish his sentences. I let *everyone* finish their sentences."

I said, "But you just interrupted me in the middle of my sentence."

She shot back, "I did *not!*"

I said, "Try not to argue. You will learn faster if you don't argue."

"I'm *not* arguing!" she interjected. Her voice was harsh and loud, her face contorted.

I said, "Blanche, you are arguing right now. You are arguing with me."

"I'm not either!" she shouted.

"And you are shouting. Why are you shouting? You'll disturb others outside."

Her voice filled with violence. She almost screamed in my face, "*I'm not either shouting!*"

Now Blanche had lost her sensitivity for what she was doing and for what that did to those around her. She didn't know where she was. She didn't know what was going on. She didn't even know the difference between an argument and a discussion. She was unaware of her own facial expression and her own voice tone. She was oblivious to her own offensiveness. She knew only her own misery, and was insensitive to anyone else's.

Later on, I tried to teach her how to take turns, letting others say what they had to say. I tried to show her that there are signals that people give with their eyes and their voices, beyond their words, that tell one that it is his turn to talk and their turn to listen. I tried to teach her these signals so that she could talk with her husband.

She said, "I already know exactly when to take my turn with Harry."

I was encouraged, and I said, "Good, Blanche. What are the signals? How do you know when it is your turn?"

"Well," she thought a minute, "when Harry takes a deep breath—like that—why, that's my signal, and I just jump right in and start talking!"

Would that Blanche were an isolated instance, but unfortunately she is not. There are many, many like her. Indeed, her situation would be comic were it not so tragic. I might have talked to her for an eternity about sensing the feelings of other people, about knowing their hearts, about reading the lines in their faces or seeing the lights in their eyes. She would only have said, "I didn't see any light in their eyes. What light in their eyes? There wasn't any light in their eyes."

But there are people who are sensitively aware, whose sensitivity to the deep reality around them is sharp and able. Such people are immediately aware of the difference between an argument and a discussion. They are aware of deep realities behind and beyond a person's words and outward actions. They can tell much by looking in a person's face, or by listening to his voice tone. They can sense another's feelings; they know long before he cries that he is hurt. They see beyond the external appearances of having and doing; they reach inward to the soul's "presence," to the actual heavenly being inside the body beyond the clutter and distractions of the world.

A very sensitive young girl named Sally came one day with some problems that were new to her, but old to me. She started to tell me something that I had heard many, many times, so many that I could have answered her questions in my sleep. As she began to talk, I began to think about my cow. I live outside of town on a little farm, and I have a fine Jersey cow that was about ready to calve. I began to think about my cow and listen to Sally at the same time. But suddenly, Sally stopped talking, right in the middle of her sentence, and said, "The doors in your eyes just closed."

I said, "Sally, can you see the doors in my eyes?"

"Yes," she replied, "and they just closed."

I blushed, cleared my throat, and said, "You are right. I was thinking about my cow."

And even though I was embarrassed, I was excited by her sensitivity. She had seen the doors in my eyes, and she had seen me go out from her and shut those doors after me. She knew that I was not present in our relationship. She could tell that I was thinking about something else. I hadn't thought that she would even notice, let alone catch me at it, but she had caught me, and had even dared to tell me. She was living at a deep level of sensitivity.

The next evening I was speaking to some of the faculty of a large university. I told them about my experience with Sally, about her seeing the doors in my eyes. After I was finished with the lecture, one of the men on the faculty came up and asked me about that.

He said, "Umm—about those doors—you were just fooling about them, weren't you?"

"No," I replied, "I was very serious."

He scratched his head in a puzzled fashion, then said, "There couldn't be doors in there. There's nothing in there at all that opens or shuts. There's only a lens and a retina, and it's all solid. Where did she get doors? There's no place for anything like that in a person's eyes. And besides, even if a person did have doors in his eyes, how would they swing in or out? How could they swing open or shut at all?"

Some people are almost completely immersed in the things of this earth. They cannot go beyond what is perceivable by their physical sense. They are caught in this world's dimensions, and are unwilling, and often unable, to escape. What they can touch, see, hear, smell—whatever occupies space and has form—these to them are real; these can be handled and coped with. Whatever else one might suppose is unreal, non-existent. Quantity and accumulation become their only measures of value. But there are other dimensions equally as valid as these.

A dimension is a measurement. Within our dimensions we measure out the depth, the breadth, the length, and even the worth of our lives. As soon as the spirit of man takes on earth life, it struggles to master its new dimensional relationships. The spatial dimension swiftly predominates; near and far, under and over, rise and fall, these begin to have dominant meaning. The body, with its parts and its functions, begins to be used (and misused) to make contact with the world and other persons within its spatial reach.

Gradually a young child becomes aware of the dimension of time. Time relationships begin to have meaning. He begins to measure and arrange events that happen to him in terms of sequences, of before and after. He adopts, necessarily and conveniently, the world's measurement scale of minutes, hours, days, and years. He becomes terribly conscious of the changes that occur in his body as he grows older, and he is indoctrinated with the values the world places on these changes. Perhaps he begins to serve these changes, seeking to obtain some and to avoid others. He may begin to worship youth, or power, or socially prescribed beauty; he may seek to shape himself to some prescribed mold, exercising and padding his body, decorating and emphasizing its parts. As he comes of age, the world's dimensions of space and time may become his major dimensions and, at last, may become the only dimensions by which he measures the values of his existence.

But man's spirit did not come from a sphere so distinctly limited. That inner being of man has no age as we are able here to measure it. It has no space as we know it. At birth it climbs into its body and remains there until released by death. It cannot be measured, nor touched, nor smelled. It does not grow old, nor older, as does the physical body in which it dwells. It comes from an entirely different dimension with different systems of measurement far finer than this earth's. This may be what the Lord is talking about when he said through Isaiah, the prophet: "For my thoughts are not your thoughts, neither are your ways my ways, saith the Lord. For as the heavens are higher than the earth, so are my ways higher than your ways, and my thoughts than your thoughts." (Isaiah 55:8-9.)

The major opportunity of each spirit who takes upon himself earth life is to continue to "keep" his first estate. This means maintaining his spiritual achievement, remaining true to his original self, nourishing and increasing his spiritual inheritance of sensitivity, awareness, empathy, understanding, and love through his mortal experience. To Abraham, the Lord said, "They who keep their first estate shall be added upon; and they who keep not their first estate shall not have glory in the same kingdom with those who keep their first estate." (Abraham 3:26.)

Keeping one's first estate, maintaining one's spiritual perspective, extends past the preexistence, through this earth life, and beyond. It is a maintained condition, like skillfulness, or honesty, or love, or righteousness. If a skill is not maintained, or a virtue not kept, these lose their existence as though they never had been. In the same way, any disobedience to the commandments negates all former obedience. One must be constant. One must be faithful. One must consistently maintain his position. Keeping our first estate is a continual process, and, as the Lord explained to Abraham, it is basic to enjoying a fully successful life upon the earth.

2

Putting First Things First

We quarter our gross bodies on our poor souls, till the former eat up all the latter's substance. (Henry David Thoreau.)

One of the aims of Satan is to distract men from maintaining their first estate. Satan would imprison each of us beneath earth's dimensions of time and space. He would destroy our shining future by disturbing our initial position, our already-achieved spiritual stance. Satan would stifle sensitivity, muffle spiritual perception; he would cover men's eyes that they cannot see, and plug their ears that they cannot hear. He would level men to the lowest common denominator, smothering that precious sensitivity attained in their first estate, and thereby make it impossible for them to qualify for keeping their second estate wherein "glory shall be added upon their heads forever and ever."

The Lord has said that Satan is a liar and the father of lies. And how true this is! Satan's whole plan is to lie to us, to get us to accept his counterfeit interpretations in place of the real interpretation, which is the gospel of Jesus Christ. Basic to Satan's plan is that we should accept a counterfeit identity, a

9

"world" self, in place of our real spirit self, and that we should measure our worth in worldly ways, in appearance, in group approvals, in social achievements, and so on. He would have us believe that these things *are* our selves, our real selves. He whispers in our ears, "You go out and buy yourself some new clothes, and get some plastic hair—then you'll feel like a million bucks!" Or, "You get yourself on the pom-pom team, or get to be a cheerleader, or get the lead in the play, or lead your company in sales, or get to be the president of the board, or a leader of the people, and *then* you'll be somebody." But he never tells us that our need for worth and purpose is spiritual, that it is a continuing need from our first estate, and that these outward things that he promotes are of the earth and external to our spirits, and that therefore they can never really satisfy.

When a person is mentally ill, depressed, neurotic, or disordered in any way, it is because he is not keeping his first estate; he is not being true to his original spirit self. I know a young girl who tried to kill herself because she wasn't accepted into a certain sorority. She wasn't accepted because her body didn't fit the acceptable mold. She didn't have the right shape, or the right size, or the right face to suit that society. She was terribly hurt because her healthy clean young body didn't satisfy some others' designs. I said to her, "Jill, why did you try to kill yourself?"

She looked at me through her tears. "You know," she said. "It's because I'm no good. Nobody wants me. They never have. I'm nothing. Nothing. Nothing." She buried her face in her hands. "Nobody would have missed me if I had killed myself. Nobody cares about me. I don't matter to anybody—even my dog, in a few days, would have gone to somebody else, and forgotten me."

How worthless she felt she was! And how confused she *really* was, and hopeless! She had come to think that her body was her self. If her body was acceptable, then she was acceptable; if it failed, she had failed. But how absolutely wrong she was. Her body was really external to her real self. It was like a car, a house, or a suit of clothing. A body exists to serve the spirit that dwells in it. It is external and of the world; it is a servant to the internal reality of the soul. Because Jill had lost her original perspective, she had allowed external things to usurp control, and mental illness was the result—grinding, clashing internal warfare, tension, nervousness, "can't sleep— can't eat—hate everybody—hate myself," until finally the crowning confirmation came in her rejection by the sorority (which was another external), and she tried to take her life.

How vital it is then to have a correct self-concept! How important it is to our mental health to know our real selves, to recognize the proper purposes and places of internal and external values! Yet how often do we submit ourselves to worldly things and let them rule our lives? We even teach our children to measure their worth by such things. An elementary school counselor said to me one day, "I can see what's wrong with Johnny. He has a poor self-concept. We can fix that. We will place him in a lower reading group where he can have a lot more successes. Then he will feel better about himself."

This is confusion. The counselor confused Johnny's value as a person with his performance at reading. His idea was that Johnny would respect himself more because his performance *appeared* to be better. The counselor hoped that if he arranged things so that Johnny could appear to be a better reader, he would like himself better, would be less antagonistic and more cooperative. In reality, Johnny wouldn't like his inner self any better at all, but only his outer performance. And that, actually, was merely appearance (which is always relative and, in this case, even false).

In healthy people, performances and appearances are outward reflections of the inner self. Externals flow outward from internals. The soul is king. The spirit-self is master. In healthy people there is order and harmony. First things are first, and second things are second. Value systems cease to be relative. Integrity, love, tenderness, assertiveness, consideration, privacy, modesty, chastity are beautiful and dependable because they flow outward from the spirit. In such a dimension, self-respect is sure.

But how often we live our lives in reverse, allowing ourselves to be governed by external things! How often we see *only* these things. Our deeper sensitivities seldom are relied upon; sometimes they become so blunted and stifled that they finally die out altogether, and external things completely rule our relationships.

Try this word game with another person (or with yourself). Ask him to say the first word that pops into his head after you say the name of an object to him. Have him concentrate on saying truly the *first* word that comes to his mind. Then begin to name a few common objects: needle, thread, chair, table, house, car, and so on. After a moment of this, add to your list the names of specific persons you both know. Listen carefully to his immediate associations. You will find that nearly all the responses are mainly concerned with externals: hard, angry, happy, joker, cute, sexy, dumb, skinny, strong, fat, black, white, smart, old, rich, big spender, tight, dentist, teacher, secretary, American, French, and so on. All the responses will be descriptive, and almost all of these will be concerned with externals. If you say his own name to him, he will respond, most of the time with externals.

Most people see themselves and the world around them in such terms. The people they know are judged and valued according to their appearances and performances. They learn this when they are children.

A few years ago I was in St. Louis at an inservice training session for elementary school teachers. As part of the training program some of the teachers were called out of the audience to take part in a little skit in which several nine-year-old children came out on the stage and pretended that it was the first day of school. Around the neck of each child hung a clean white cardboard sign upon which was printed in large black letters: I AM LOVABLE AND CAPABLE.

The children had been instructed before they came out on the stage that they were to use the signs to tell the audience how they felt inside during the interaction. "When someone treats you in a way that says you are lovable and capable—that you are interesting, good, and beautiful, that you have good sense, and that he likes to be with you and loves you—then you are to smile and show with your eyes that you are very happy; you are to rub your sign and say 'Ummmmm, good.' But when someone puts you down, or hurts you, or says something mean to you that makes you feel bad, or that tells you that you can't figure anything out by yourself, then you are to tear off a piece of your sign."

One little boy came out on the stage, and the teacher put her arm around him. He rubbed his sign gently.

"Hi, Tim," the teacher said. "Did you have a good summer?"

"Oh, I had a wonderful summer," he replied. "We went to Disneyland. We went on everything! We had so much fun. It was a wonderful summer."

The teacher listened, then talked some more. And the little boy continued to stroke his sign. After a while the teacher said, "Well, that was nice, but we had better get down to work." Then she took her arm from around his waist and put it on his shoulder, pushing him gently toward a chair at a corner table. "Come over here, Tim, and we'll see if you can read any better now than you did last year." And she made a wry face as she said it.

The little boy slipped out from under her guiding hand and turned toward her. He held up his sign, then ripped off a big chunk of it—about a third of the word *capable*—and handed it to her. It was funny, and the audience laughed. But there was terrible truth in the scene on the stage—the little boy, part of his beautiful new sign torn now and jagged, his *capable* partly destroyed, and the teacher beside him, blankly fiddling with the torn part of the child's sign, wondering what to do with it now that she had it, and probably wondering what she had done to get it in the first place.

What she had done was tell the boy he was stupid. Had she been confronted with that, she would have said that was not what she meant at all. But the little boy had heard her words; he had heard the demeaning tone of her voice, and he had seen the wry expression on her face out of the corner of his eye. He had gotten her message. These signals all told him that she didn't think he was lovable at all and certainly not very capable. Not only was he stupid, but he was also a personal embarrassment to her. She had told him all of this with her voice tone and her facial expression. And so he had ripped a piece from his sign.

We communicate with each other through three major means: body posture and facial expression, voice tone, and words. One study showed that in most communication, 55 percent of a message is conveyed by the person's body posture and facial expression and 38 percent is conveyed by voice tone. Only 7 percent is conveyed by the specific words spoken! Little children, having only recently learned words, rely heavily upon nonverbal signals for communication.

And children are *very* sensitive and perceptive. In the skit in St. Louis, one little girl raised her hand and said to the teacher, "Miss Jones, may I please go to the bathroom?"

"Of course, Sally dear," the teacher replied in her best first-day-at-school, I-will-be-patient-with-you tone of voice. "Go out the door and down the hall about halfway. You will see two green doors. BOYS is on one door, and GIRLS is on the other door. Now Sally, you go in the door with GIRLS on it."

Little Sally stood up, turned toward the audience, and ripped her sign in half!

Her action really upset the teacher. Miss Jones ran over to the director of the skit. "What did I do wrong?" she cried. "Why did Sally rip her sign at me like that? I was *so* nice to her—"

Sally marched over to the teacher, holding the two jagged parts of her pretty white sign in front of her. With the first part, she pointed to the second part. "Miss Jones," she said, "capable, capable, capable on the label, label, label." And then she placed her hands on her hips and announced firmly, "I can go to the girls' room all by myself."

Too often, much that parents and teachers say to children, both verbally and nonverbally, is negative, telling them in one way or another that they are not lovable and not capable. Seemingly, to most grown-ups, the child's external appearances and performances are more important than his inside feelings as a new human being and his actual value as a child of God. Many adults indoctrinate the child to believe this also. Often this indoctrination is quite cruel. Some grown-ups say, verbally and nonverbally, "We don't like you. You wet the bed." And the child feels inside, "But I am still a good person even when I wet the bed." But the message comes back, "You are not. You stink."

But it is *not* the child who stinks. It is his body that stinks, or it is his bed that stinks, or his clothing. We, as parents, may not like his wetting the bed; that is merely a performance. But we ought to love his beautiful self, and we ought to tell him so. We ought to teach him the relationship between what he *does* and what he *is*. He should be taught that what he does is the *result* of what he is, not the reverse.

What happens when a little child is told over and over again, in many different ways, that she is not capable, that she can't find the bathroom by herself and can't take care of her own needs? Soon she won't say anymore, "Capable, capable, capable on the label, label, label." She will believe the lies that come from such infallible sources, and soon she will say, "Will you take me to the bathroom? I can't take care of myself." Soon she will lose contact with her preexistent confidence. She will cease to know her beautiful inside self, and cease to trust it to do its assigned jobs. She will begin to rely solely upon the world's counterfeits.

In our world, body is king. A person can buy fake worth by having his body fit a certain mold, by arranging his body in certain ways, or by doing certain things with his body. Age, race, color, size, shape, use, sex—all have become conditions of inner worth, conditions for acceptance and status. In the world, status is happiness, or at least it is thought to be.

But happiness, worth, joy, purpose, meaning—these are all internal things. In their highest development, they are spiritual. Appropriately providing for them is the job of the inside self. And the inside self is capable. It is able to do this if allowed. Worth is built into the spirit in the preexistence. Worth does not have to be earned all over again here on earth. Man has worth simply because he is a child of God, a human being, a shining spirit self with a marvelous body and a right to grow and become. Worth is programmed into man before he is born, and, as the self grows in mortality (if it is *allowed* to grow), man becomes even more confidently and sensitively aware of that fact.

But suppose the spirit self is not allowed to grow as it ought? Suppose it is muffled and stifled and covered over with the refuse of the world? Suppose it is not given the nourishment it needs? Then it cannot do its job. It can't provide for the person's spiritual needs—his needs of worth and purpose that lead him to joy and happiness. Externals appear to him to be all there is, and he turns to them anxiously. Body and performance become the main agents of supply for what the stifled spirit is no longer allowed to provide.

The body is deceptively able to do this substitute task. A person can obtain all kinds of counterfeit worth with his body and its performances. Such feelings come when bidden by way of beauty contests, sports, drugs, alcohol, sex, food. They even come with illness. One very prominent physician told me that "seventy percent of all hospitalized illness is psychogenic." By *psychogenic* he meant that the illness had its beginnings in some psychological disorder or disharmony.

We learn early in childhood that if we are sick at school, we can get special treatment and consideration. We learn that if we say, "I think I have appendicitis," the nurse will tell us immediately, "Oh, you need to go right home. We will call your mother. She will come and get you and take care of you." But if we say, "I hurt inside. My parents are fighting and quarreling, and I am upset. I worry all the time wondering if they are going to get a divorce," the nurse will say, "Oh, well, you will get over it. You'd better go back to class and get your work done." In our society, body rules. We learn as children that if something is wrong with our bodies, we can get out of uncomfortable situations and into more comfortable ones. At the university around final examination time, illness increases considerably. Students suffer from stomach pains, sore throats, aches and pains of all kinds and variations. This is because illness is a legitimate way to postpone final examinations. Illness is an acceptable way out.

It is the same situation, actually, when illness serves to buy substitute love. A sick body can provide love and attention without damage to the ill person's ego. I had a lady patient who fell and broke her leg. After her leg healed and it came time for her to give up her crutches, she rebelled. "Oh, please," she moaned, "do I have to give up my crutches? I've never had so much attention in all my life! People move out of my way when I come along the sidewalk. They never used to do that. And when I come into a room, people say, 'Would you like to sit here, Mabel?' 'What can I do to help you, Mabel?' They never used to do that. And people ask me now how I feel. They never used to care. Can't I keep my crutches? Please?"

Mabel had learned that she could use a hurt body to secure a kind of substitute love. She had learned that she could get the attention she had never had by substituting the value of her body for the value of her real self.

Body value creates new dimensions. It allows people to attribute worth to themselves because of their body shape, or color, or kind, or size. "I look younger than Mary" (therefore I am better than Mary). "I look great in a bikini" (therefore I am better than Joanne, who wouldn't dare be seen in one). "I have beautiful eyes." "I have shiny hair." "My muscles are bigger than his." "I'm taller than her father." "I'm black." "I'm white." And so on. It is an endless self congratulation, and all based upon false measures.

But false or not, people continue to measure themselves by their bodies. A lady looks in the mirror and sees that her hair is beginning to turn gray. "Oh," she sighs, "I'm getting old." And she begins to worry. After a while, she goes to her hairdresser and has her hair dyed back to its youthful color. But what is she really worried about? She is worried because she believes that her worth, her value to other people, is tied up with her youthfulness. She believes that as she gets older, she will lose the love and respect of her loved ones. But if this is actually so, it is because they, as well as she, believe the same lie. They are all building their lives upon false measurements, and they will all pay the consequences. The woman is covering up one lie (that young bodies rate more love than old bodies) with another (that *her* body is not old, but is still young). She is teaching her children and others that the first lie matters, and that the second one is justified. Later on, she may wonder why her children lie and deceive to get what they want. She may even wonder where they learned to do this; she will deny vehemently that she taught it to them.

The body was made to be the temple wherein the heavenly being of man should dwell. It is the house that the spirit self occupies while it passes through mortal experience. The body was not meant to be the god of the spirit, nor was it meant to be worshipped and served by the spirit. The body was not intended to be the means for providing worth and love to man's inner being. These needs are spiritual needs. When the body is forced to do the work of the spirit, both body and spirit lose their real identities, and maladjustment, despair, dejection, mental illness, and often tragedy result—for the body cannot satisfy these non-body demands.

First things must be placed first, and second things, second. The spirit is first. It must rule. The body, and all the external things it is able to do, is second. It must obey the spirit. External things, such as appearances and performances, should flow from the spirit, from the inside self. They should be inseparable results of the first-estate identity of each individual.

3

Be Not Deceived

When you are overtaken in a fault, or commit an overt act unthinkingly; when you are full of evil passion, and wish to yield to it, then stop and let the spirit which God has put into your tabernacle take the lead. If you do that, I will promise that you will overcome all evil, and obtain eternal lives. (Brigham Young.)

A new commandment I give unto you, That ye love one another; as I have loved you, that ye also love one another. By this shall all men know that ye are my disciples, if ye have love one to another. (John 13:34-35.)

To be a true disciple of Christ is to live wholly and magnificently as he lived, loving perfectly as he loved. Jesus' love was a love without guile, beyond selfishness, for he saw all things in the bright, true light of the spiritual perspective. He saw through men's brittle defensive walls, past their blunted sensitivities, their selfish blindnesses, to the essential and original spirit self deep inside. He commanded his followers to do the same. "Follow me," he said over and over again to his disciples in Jerusalem—and to the Nephite twelve he admonished, "Therefore, what manner of men ought ye to be? Verily I say

19

unto you, even as I am." (3 Nephi 27:27.)

Such a life requires acts of genuine service and love; such intimate performances must flow from deep inside. One cannot force love. Love that is not genuine, love that is exploitation or perhaps merely duty, is detectable immediately by sensitive persons—and it is resented, for being lied to is always offensive to the God-given spirits of men.

One mother, after hearing a discussion about how mothers should supply love to their children, determined that before her fourteen-year-old son went to school in the morning, she would give him a hug. She wanted to prove to him and to herself that she was a good mother. That next morning, as she tried to hug him, he rejected her. But she was determined to give him a hug, and she chased him around the kitchen table and even out the back door. He ran away from her—down the driveway, down the long sidewalk, and around the corner beyond her sight. She stood abandoned in the driveway, crying. She was so frustrated that she went into the house and called the school counselor and told him the whole story, how her son was mean to her and rejected her when she had tried to love him.

The concerned counselor called the boy privately out of class and tried to talk to him. He asked the boy why he had acted that way toward his mother. The boy looked at him quizzically, then he said, "Mr. Jones, do you know the difference between a hug that gives and a hug that takes?"

The counselor, who was not a very sensitive person himself, replied, "No."

And the boy said quickly, "That's what I thought."

School counselors aren't all so insensitive. Many of them are highly sensitive people who do know the difference between a hug that gives and a hug that takes. But this particular counselor had allowed his own feelings of worth and responsibility to become confused with the distraught mother's feelings of inadequacy, and he had taken on a task that the boy sensed immediately he was not able to handle. It is a perfect example of doing things for the wrong reasons. The counselor did not call the boy in to find out how the boy felt, but rather to scold the boy for not making his mother feel better. And the mother had not wanted to hug the boy because her heart was filled with love for him, but rather to prove to herself that she was doing her job as a mother according to specifications. Her action is an example of performance being forced to represent what was not entirely there. The boy sensed that his mother's affection was mainly to fill *her* need. Her performance of love was not what it appeared to be. It did not flow from her spiritual self, purely, freely, without guile. It was partly a lie, meant to deceive both him and her. The young boy may not have understood all of this, but he felt it, sensitively and intuitively, and he turned from it because it was uncomfortable to him.

Little children often dream that lions are gobbling them up. Sometimes they dream that their mother or father is gobbling them up. In the scriptures, ancient prophets have prophesied that in the last days parents would devour their children. Perhaps this means that in the last days parents will be so inadequate in themselves, having lost much of their original meaning and purpose, that they will grasp at their children and devour their lives, saying, "*You* will be my purpose and my meaning! *You* are what I have to live for!" But the eternal spirit self inside the child fights back, striving to keep its independence, struggling with all its might to keep itself from being devoured. At the close of that unhappy interview with his school counselor, the fourteen-year-old boy who had refused his mother's hug tried to explain. "When my mom hugs me, I feel terrible—I don't like it at all." Then, seeing that he was not understood, he turned angrily and cried out, "I wouldn't hug my mother if she were the last woman on earth!"

Genuine love is not a service nor a duty. It does not exist to prove anything to anyone, though many times, when we are lost and disoriented, we may try to make it do so.

A very empty and desperate young woman came to my office a while back. She said, "My life is miserable. I hate my marriage. I hate the man I married. I hate my life. I stay home and I clean the bedroom. I clean the bathroom. I clean the toilets. I clean the kitchen. I fix the food. I hate it! I hate it! In the next twenty years I will fix 21,900 meals for that man. I'm not going to do it. I hate it. I *hate* it! I HATE IT!" And she started to cry. She covered her face with her hands and sobbed. "Oh, I am so empty—why should I live at all? What is to become of me?" She sat there sobbing; then, quite suddenly, she stopped. She lifted her head, wiped the tears from her eyes, and smiled. Confidence lighted her face. "I know what I'll do," she said. "I'll have a baby!"

I couldn't help smiling. "Lucky baby," I said.

But she didn't understand. "What do you mean?" she asked.

"Well, Joyce, what are you going to *do* with that baby when you get it?"

She thought a moment, then replied, "A baby will give me purpose. It will give me meaning. Then I will be somebody. I won't be so dependent on my husband. I'll have the baby!"

And there it was. What she meant to do was deliberately have a baby so that she could gobble it up, stuff it down into her giant emptiness, and make it do the job her inside self was no longer able to do. In the years to come that little baby would grow up fighting for its life. Through the years, as the battle lines formed, he would begin to sense his mother was his enemy, a cannibal who sought to gobble him up for her selfish satisfaction. And when one morning she might try to hug him, to fill up her emptiness—he would run wildly from her, shouting angrily at anyone who would listen, "I don't care! I wouldn't hug her if she were the last person on earth!"

This sort of thing happens often. One mother came to me about her daughter who was thirteen, pregnant, and not married. "I can't understand it," she said. "Linda is my whole life, and now she does this to me. All she wants to do is to get out of the house. Well, now she's going."

But why does Linda want to get out of her mother's house? In this case, the answer is obvious. Linda wants out so that her mother won't gobble her up any more and make her life her mother's purpose and meaning. Linda's mother *gives* in order to *get.* She offers Linda a nice sweet hug, but Linda feels only revulsion and despair, and she cries out, "You keep away from me." Linda's mother's hug is a hug that takes; it is not a hug that gives.

Now hugs, in and of themselves, are neither good nor bad; they are merely external performances. They are good if they flow outward as genuine expressions of deep internal feelings, but like anything else, they are bad if they are misused—if they are used to deceive, to lie, to manipulate another person, or to compensate for one's own feelings of deficiency.

Such use of external performances results in extreme damage to a child. It is at home that a child's deepest concepts of himself are first formed, yet the forming process continues all of his life. He comes to this earth with a potential self-concept that is divine, pure, and adequate, and that if nourished with genuine love and positive recognition, can bring great joy and security throughout his earth-life experience. But often, as soon as he is born he is immediately confronted with counterfeit love relationships, and he begins desperately to set up defense systems to protect himself. Gradually he develops a "world" self-concept, shaped by the treatment he receives from those around him; he begins to cover his precious, beautiful self with increasingly deep layers of his more acceptable world self. A lifetime of this process can result in unhappiness, frustration, futility, and mental illness.

It can happen so simply. One Sunday morning a young girl goes to Sunday School. There the teacher of her class teaches her that she is a child of God. She tells the young girl, "You come from another dimension where there is no time and no space as we know them here." She teaches her that she is divine, that she has an inborn sensitivity to divine things. She teaches her that she is not alone, that she can talk to her Father in heaven freely, without any barriers, simply by prayer, and that he will hear her and will answer her if she will listen. Her teacher tells her that before she came to earth, when she was with her Father in heaven, she used to move on a beam of light, and that she had great power and beauty. She teaches her that she was, and still is, a glorious personage, able, sweet, and unutterably precious. And she reads to her from the eighth psalm where the psalmist is filled with wonder at what the Lord had done for each one of his children: "For thou hast made him a little lower than the angels, and hast crowned him with glory and honour." (Psalm 8:5.) And the young girl believes what her teacher tells her.

She comes home floating on a cloud. "I am beautiful. I am a glorious personage. I'm noble. I'm divine. I came here on a seventy-year assignment from another dimension. When my body stops, my inside self is going to go back." She just loves it! It is wonderful! It seems so right! She comes home singing.

Her mother is preparing the Sunday dinner. Harried, rushed, her mother says, "Julie, hurry now! Change your clothes. Set the table. We have to be over to Uncle Ned's home in forty minutes. Hurry! Hurry! We don't want to be late." And Julie hurries to her room, begins to change her clothes, throws her stuff around, gets interested in a magazine article, and starts to read. In about ten minutes her mother storms into the room. She has a terrible look on her face. She sees Julie, sitting on the bed, half-dressed, reading. Her mother yells, "What are you doing? I told you to get your clothes changed! I told you to come and set the table!"

The girl looks up, troubled. She sets up her defenses. "Oh! Sorry, mother. I got interested in this article. I'll be right there. I'll change my clothes." She gets up warily.

But her mother is so mad and frustrated that she slaps her across the face. "Oh, shut up! You've already made us late! Oh, you make me so mad!" She glares at the girl and then turns and slams back down into the kitchen.

The young girl stands alone in her bedroom. Her face smarts, and there is a ringing in her ear. Softly she says to herself, "I thought I was a glorious person—a little lower than the angels, crowned with glory and honor—but my mother slaps me in the face and tells me to shut up!" Then she ponders the age-old question: "Who is right about me, my mother or my Sunday School teacher? My teacher tells me I am a glorious person, but my mother treats me like a worm. Which one is right? What *am* I, anyway?"

Deep down inside herself Julie senses that what her teacher has told her is the truth, and that the way her mother is treating her is unjust and wrong, but it's hard for a young girl to make judgments against her mother. There is little else she can do in that moment but accept her mother's negative treatment as truth and catalog it with the rest of her growing world-self-concepts and adapt to these so that she can get along with the people in the world around her.

Julie, like most people, needs to find sources of genuine, positive love matching her true identity; otherwise she may be brainwashed into believing the negative counterfeits that are constantly being piled upon her. Otherwise she may develop inferiority feelings about being Julie. She has been convinced that Julie is not lovable and not capable. Instead she is inade-quate, helpless, unsatisfactory, and certainly *not* beautiful. It hurts to be criticized, to be negated, to be treated contrary to one's true identity. And as Julie begins to believe the world's counterfeits, she will also begin to form a cover, a style of acting, perhaps a whole elaborate system of psychological de-fenses, so that she can tolerate her pain and disappointment. Slowly she will begin to bury her true, original, beautiful self deep inside, covering it over with the world's deceptions and Satan's lies, and then covering that with a brittle armor of poses and behaviors that, at last, she may come to believe is her true and only self.

There are those whose composition has become so over-whelmingly negative that only the smallest smidgen of positive self can be discerned. These people are very unhappy, and usually those around them are miserable also.

A man came into my office one day. He was unhappy. He said that his wife weighed 247 pounds. He said, "I told Wilma when I married her that if she got fat I would leave her. I told her I would divorce her if she put on a pile of weight, and now she has." Then he made a great statement that told me that he had married only his wife's body, that he had never known her soul. He said, "That body she is going around in now is not the body that I contracted for."

I said to him, "Harry, sit down. You know that it could be partly your problem that Wilma weighs 247 pounds."

He looked at me angrily. "What do you mean by that?"

"I mean that possibly, if you stayed home sometimes and gave Wilma the positive love she needs, she wouldn't be eating food for love."

So we talked about this whole picture for some time, and I tried to show him how Wilma needed positive nourishment to overcome all the negative conditioning she had piled over her beautiful self. He listened and finally nodded his head in comprehension. Then he took his appointment card, turned it over, and drew a picture on it. "Here is Wilma," he said, and he drew a tiny speck so small that I could hardly see it. "And here is her garbage pile," and he drew a large circle around the speck, darkening with his pencil the thick layer around the tiny speck. He continued, "And here is her outside armor, her defenses," and he drew another heavy circle about the first one, making it thick and dark. "Now," he said, "I would be glad to stay home and love her if I could find her beneath all that fat!"

There are those persons who, like Wilma, have covered themselves over so completely, so efficiently, so protectively, that even though one probes with all patience and strength, he may not be able to find and reach that tiny remaining speck of spirit light.

But there are also those in the world who have not covered themselves over, who are more positive than negative, who have had adequate positive nurture from their first appearance upon the earth, who have very thin layers of worldly padding and very small loads of garbage, and only narrow defensive barriers that cover only small pain. These people are sensitive; they sparkle and shine. They have great power and great beauty. Their beautiful selves shine through their thin world layers as the bright sun shines through wispy layers of earth's morning clouds. When such a person comes near, we feel we have known him before—and we feel safe with him; we are able to love him without guile as we loved each other in our first estate before we left our Father's house and took on mortality and the test of this earth life.

Such people are congruent. They have learned how to keep external things in harmony with internal reality. In their lives, the inside self is in control of the outside world. In other words, such a person is keeping or maintaining his first estate in the midst of his experience in his second estate. In him, both estates are being brought together in a mutually contributive relationship that brings honor and glory inevitably to the spirit accomplishing it.

And the spirit *can* accomplish it. It *is* able. The spirit, the inside self that is in every man and woman born to this earth, has wonderful qualities. It is lovable and capable. It is interesting; it is exciting; it is thrilling. It has great magnetic power; it is attractive and powerful. It is intelligent, precious, sensitively aware. It is genuine and exceedingly beautiful. It has unbelievable powers. It can communicate across space without mechanical aids. It has extrasensory perception. It can read minds. It can feel feelings. It can interpret thoughts. It can look into people's faces and see things that perhaps the other person's outside self does not want seen. It has a photographic memory. It records everything that happens to it here on earth. Under certain circumstances (hypnotism, for instance), it can recall things the outside self did not even recognize were happening. It can make right decisions. It can predict the future. It has fantastic potentials inherited from its first dimension far beyond the narrow confines of its present earthly home.

And to those who listen, it speaks assurance and direction, constantly, and without fail. Each of us needs to learn to recognize its voice. We need to become sensitive to its communication. I know a young man who said that one afternoon his teacher gave him the key to the stockroom of his school and asked him to get a new pencil sharpener for their schoolroom. As he unlocked the stockroom and entered, he saw ten or twelve brand new pencil sharpeners on the shelf before him. Suddenly a voice within him said, "Say, Eric, why don't you just take one of those pencil sharpeners for your room at home? Your room at home doesn't have a pencil sharpener, and you've always wanted one there just like the one at school—" And then another voice inside him said, "Eric, you can't take other people's things like that. How would you like someone to take your things?" And another voice said, "Why don't you just borrow one? You could take it back after a while." And then another voice, said, "Maybe you could buy one from the school. Maybe you could get it for a cheap price." And the boy stood there looking at those shiny new pencil sharpeners and wondering what to do. Which voice should he follow? Which advice was best? Later he said to me, "How can I know which one of those voices is the real me?" And as we talked about it, he began to see that there are certain signs or signals, certain keys, that seem always to accompany and identify the voice of the real self.

The most prominent and dependable of these keys is that the voice of the real self, the spirit, is always considerate of other people. It is never selfish. It is never taking. It never seeks possession. It doesn't rationalize. It doesn't maneuver. It has no hidden agenda, no ulterior motive. Its message is clean and simple, direct and uncomplicated. A second key is that it usually speaks in a quick, quiet flash. It sweeps across the mind spontaneously, unbidden, immediate. It comes from the heart, not the head. It is not cognitive; it is not thought out. It is usually kind but firm, and it has great tenderness and power. In most normal situations, in healthy people, its voice usually speaks first or second among the other voices.

The other voices we hear originate in the world self, formed of the layers and defenses fashioned to satisfy the world and Satan's deceptions. These voices are basically inconsiderate of other people. They are usually selfish. They seek gain. They rationalize, maneuver, and manipulate. They are cognitive in that they are mental efforts to get something. In all their various forms, they most often flash second, presenting answers, excuses, alternatives to the primary message of the real self. Their various messages are often not coherent; they sometimes even argue with each other. Their positions are often complicated and unsure. Under pressure, they may be frantic and violent.

But the real self, the spirit, the heavenly being that dwells within each one of us, that indeed *is* each one of us, is not frantic nor violent. It is not defensive. It does not rationalize nor turn this way and that. It knows truth and is committed to it from a reality beyond the dimensions of this world's time and space.

I have read many accounts of people who have died, people who have been declared clinically dead, but who have come back to life. These persons described how it feels to leave the body, to emerge from under layers of mortality into the bright light of an almost forgotten spiritual reality. None of these accounts are exactly alike, but they contain striking similarities. The person feels himself dying; he is aware that he is leaving his body, and he sees his empty body, often with doctors and nurses or spectators gathered around it. He feels wonderfully free and easy, released from the earth. He floats weightless around the scene, completely comfortable, filled with indescribably beautiful feelings, more gentle, more loving, more powerful than his imagination has ever conceived. He finds himself moving away from his body, along a roadway or passageway, and he sometimes sees relatives or friends who have already died; he communicates with them nonverbally through the beautiful, warm, loving spirit that seems to surround him and fill him. At the end of the passageway he meets a personage of great light who seems a personification of all this powerful beauty; this person asks him, again beyond specific language, what he has done of worth in his life. He is shown quick flashbacks of his life to help him in this evaluation. The being of light asks him what he has learned, and specifically, whether he has learned to love other people. The "dead" person feels no condemnation in this, but only a wonderful, secure feeling of great all-surpassing love that fills him and satisfies him beyond anything he has known.

Reluctantly, these persons returned to their earthly bodies.

They had little wish to come back to the gross dimensions of earth life after they had felt again the overwhelming love and beauty and power of their spiritual estate. The words of Jesus now had new meaning to them: "A new commandment I give unto you, That ye love one another; as I have loved you." (John 13:34.)

Genuine love is the first law of heaven; it is the basis for all successful living. Love nourishes the powerful spirit being that is our real self, our real identity, and that dwells within our earthly bodies. Our great challenge and opportunity in earth life is to build upon this, to remember who we are, keeping our first estate, and living our mortal lives, our second estate, in that glorious light. To accomplish this well is the grand purpose of our whole earthly experience.

and temporary achievements cannot satisfy our internal need for absolute purpose and worth. Our real self knows that externals alone are fake and of the earth. It knows that true happiness is internal and spiritual and has its roots beyond this world's dimensions.

Our free agency is a gift from our heavenly parents. That inborn right to make our own choices was given to each one of us before we were born so that we could truly *be* free by willing consciously and independently to *be* so, and then working diligently to attain it. Satan would take this right of intelligent choice away from us. He would enslave us. Our Father in heaven would do just the opposite. He would provide us with opportunity and means to grow and attain the same powerful liberty that he has attained, a liberty of absolute power with great glory. It is that great absolute liberty, sure and secure, to which each one of us has been called. It comes when our lives are conducted under the direction and control of our real selves. True liberty results inevitably as we grow and expand in our second estate, keeping the already-achieved balance of our first estate. True liberty happens as we live in mortality in harmony with the spiritual reality of our real selves.

Inside each one of us, the war in heaven is never over. Inside us, whether we are aware of it or not, there is a constant struggle between our real self and our substitute world self. All of our thoughts and actions reflect this. What we think and do is determined by the way we weigh our values, external and internal. The ratio varies dependent upon our view of our needs. Sometimes our decisions are based upon a consideration of perhaps 80 percent external values and only 20 percent internal ones; at other times our decisions may be made up of 80 percent internal values and only 20 percent external ones.

Ideally, our external values should flow from our internal values, and our spirit self should be the master of all. Happiness occurs when we get our inside values and outside values congruent. Performances and appearances are simply outward reflections of the controlling self. When our spirit self is in control, peace, order, and harmony will be in our lives; when it is not, conflict, disorder, and disharmony will result.

Paul the apostle, continuing his letter to the Galatians, expressed this clearly:

"I mean this: if you are guided by the Spirit you will not fulfill the desires of your lower nature. That nature sets its desires against the Spirit, while the Spirit fights against it. They are in conflict with one another. . . .

"Anyone can see the kind of behavior that belongs to the lower nature: fornication, impurity, and indecency; idolatry and sorcery; quarrels, a contentious temper, envy, fits of rage, selfish ambitions, dissensions, party intrigues, and jealousies; drinking bouts, orgies, and the like. I warn you, as I warned you before, that those who behave in such ways will never inherit the kingdom of God.

"But the harvest of the Spirit is love, joy, peace, patience, kindness, goodness, fidelity, gentleness, and self-control. . . . If the Spirit is the source of our life, let the Spirit also direct our course." (Galatians 5:16-25. The New English Bible, Oxford University Press, 1961.)

It seemed obvious to the apostle Paul that if one desires to be happy, he must discern between the voice of the sure inner self, the spirit within, which is the receiver of the Holy Spirit, and the subtle misleading voices of the substitute self, which can rightly be called our "lower nature," the lusts and wants of our flesh.

Every child born into this world comes to this life seeking a continuation of the stable, sure beauty he knew before he came here. He seeks "love, joy, peace, patience, kindness, goodness, fidelity, gentleness, and self-control." He expects tenderness and power in all its forms to continue as they were in his heavenly family. He hopes for that "harvest of the Spirit," the attainment of those internal values that will nourish his spirit self and help him to maintain his first estate. He seeks this kind of nourishment so that he can continue to grow. He reaches out for it; he strives to find it; he searches for sources of it; and he is terribly thwarted when he cannot find it, or is unable to reach it. The seed of the spirit self seeks with indomitable energy to fulfill itself. Yet, often it is prevented from doing so. Often, in spite of violent effort, it becomes covered and stunted and almost obliterated.

In the northwest areas of the United States, in Oregon and Washington where it rains often and where lumber is a major industry, people use bark mulch to control the growth of plants around their homes. They lay heavy black plastic over the bare ground where the growth of plant life needs to be restricted. Then they cut holes in the plastic where they desire plant life to grow, and cover the plastic with six or eight inches of bark mulch. The plastic and layers of bark mulch prevent any seeds other than those in the opened areas from growing, from fulfilling their potential for becoming what they were meant to become.

In Oregon a few years ago, we had a rhododendron in our yard that didn't grow as it should have done because we had not cut away a big enough opening in the layer of black plastic. The rhododendron plant had been prevented by the plastic from receiving the sunlight and fresh air and other nourishment its roots needed to fulfill their potential. I remember scraping away the thick layers of bark mulch, laying bare the black plastic, and then pulling back that heavy layer from the earth. Beneath it, all across the surface of the earth, was a solid white mat of long runners, of long, groping, stem-like roots. Besides rhododendron roots, there were roots from many other seeds that had tried to grow. I recognized some of them by the ways in which they had sent out their shoots. Here an iris bulb sent out long pale fingers, and here a blackberry vine. Each seed had obediently begun to grow regardless of the heavy barriers above it. Each tiny plant had worked tirelessly to actualize its potential, but the thick layer of black plastic, covered with many inches of heavy damp bark mulch, had proven too formidable.

The plants could get little water and little air. They were prevented from receiving the nourishment they needed, and so each plant had searched for an opening, for a way out, for a way to live regardless—and, in the process, had changed. Instead of a blackberry bush with leaves, thorns, and juicy fruit, that seed had produced a great mass of pale thin roots and stems groping for nourishment to satisfy the driving need to stay alive. Each plant had been forced to mutate, or die. Seeking to be what it actually was, it had been forced to change itself into something that it was not so that it would not perish.

If, by chance, some of those long, white, misshapen stems did eventually find a hole in the plastic where they could come up and out, and begin to receive sunshine and air, their identities as iris, or dandelion, or blackberry plant were changed. The blackberry plant, for instance, perhaps no longer had blackberry characteristics. Some of its vines were without thorns, some without berries, some without blossoms, and some with changes in leaf shape and color. Mutation prevented the plant from maintaining its original identity.

This is what happens to the human spirit when it doesn't get the nourishment it needs, nourishment that matches its true identity as a spirit self. Even though it strives diligently to maintain its spiritual identity, to keep its first estate, it is forced by the world's dimensions to mutate and change. It finds itself overwhelmed by the things of the world, as if it were covered over with thick layers of plastic. Even so, it reaches out with a powerful, insatiable drive to find the nourishment it ought to have. It sends long, fragile runners out in all directions, seeking the nourishment that it needs. Intelligently, it begins to ascertain where it might receive the nourishment it must have to remain alive. And in this process it too mutates and changes.

The substitute self, or the world self, is the mutation that occurs. It is the substitute that develops within the restrictions and frustrations, the inhibitions and thwartings, that come to all of us who accept earth life.

The variation in our reliance upon this mutation self, as balanced against our real self, is a revealing formula. Some of us are 20-80 people—20 percent real self and 80 percent mutation self. Others are 40-60 people. Some few are 90-10 people. The ratio depends upon how much we *understand*, and *control*, our relationships with our mutation selves.

It's not difficult to discern the general balance of this ratio, especially if one identifies his sources of nourishment—his love supplies. One may ask himself: "What do I *relate to* in myself and in others? What do I like about myself? What, to me, is *me*? What gives me worth?" Questions like these point out one's sources of character nourishment. They reveal the targets toward which one is striving to grow. If these targets are internal in value, they relate to the real spirit self. If, on the other hand, they are external in value, they relate to the mutation or world self.

It's also very revealing to ask, "What do others relate to in me?"—for it is a fact that other people relate to whatever we relate to in ourselves. Unavoidably, our gropings toward our value targets reveal our nourishment needs. In time, our efforts toward external targets signal and advertise what kinds of substitute nourishment we have mutated to accept.

A young girl came into my office one day, extremely upset. She sat down in the chair opposite me and began to tell me why she was so disturbed. As she did so she dabbed at her eyes with the corner of her handkerchief and smoothed her blouse around her waist, pulling it tight from her shoulders to her skirt.

"Oh," she said, "you men! I can't stand you men. Everywhere I go men ogle at me and gaze at me. I feel like some kind of a birthday cake or something just waiting to be eaten!"

"Well, Jackie," I said, "after all, you take great pains to be a very attractive girl."

She blushed prettily and fiddled with the buttons of her blouse. "Thank you," she said. Then suddenly she burst out with, "I can't help it if I'm attractive." She fussed with her short skirt, pulling it this way and that, trying to make it longer than it really was.

I said to her, "Your skirt *is* pretty short, Jackie."

She flared back at me, "I know it is! I know it's short."

She started to dab at her eyes again. After a while she said, "I don't have a very pretty face, and I know that I don't have a very interesting personality." She waited, but I said nothing. She went on. "People don't talk to me as they talk to other people." She paused again, but I simply listened. Then she said abruptly, "But I do have pretty legs. That's what I have. If I wore long skirts I would have nothing, don't you see?"

What Jackie said was that one of the targets she had found to shoot toward for a love supply was her body—specifically, her socially acceptable, well-shaped legs. Her legs were what *she had decided* she liked about herself. They made her feel good about being Jackie. She had even begun to mutate, to believe that her legs *were* Jackie. And her signals invited others to relate to her in the same way she related to herself.

Jackie felt resentment because she sensed that the substitute love nourishment she was receiving was not the genuine nourishment she sought. She sought for real love, for a recognition of her internal worth as a person. She longed to have people relate to her character, to her personal worth, but they rarely got a chance to get that close to her. Her legs were always in the way! Inwardly she felt this confusion but was too cluttered to understand or know what to do. And so she continued as she was, blindly sending her futile shoots along the same routes toward the same false targets—and sick boys continued to look, and she continued to accept their cheap attention for the genuine love she longed so much to have. Of course, her real self was offended—that heavenly being within her had every right to be.

A young boy who was on drugs said to me one morning, "Well, I finally did what my mother told me to do."

I said, "What was that?"

"Well," he said, "I finally got a date with Kathryn. But it was a mistake, a complete mistake. It was a miserable evening. That Kathryn is a real loser. She didn't turn me on all evening. I don't know what it is about those society girls my mother wants me to go with, but every time I get anywhere near one of them it's perfectly lousy. I just don't get along with that kind of people."

What he was really saying was that he could not relate to Kathryn's value system. Her love targets were not acceptable to him, and likewise, the targets that he reached for were not acceptable to her. Of course they couldn't get along together. She could not nourish *his* mutated substitute self, and he could not nourish *her* mutated substitute self. In their blindness, each blamed the other without realizing that the discrepancy was a mutual one.

A young girl sat across from me crying, saying, "I don't know why it is. I'm never able to get a date with the kind of boy I'd really like to marry. Good boys just don't date me. The only boys I ever attract are ones who try to take me to bed. I'll never marry the kind of man I want to marry. I'm just that kind of a girl, I guess, and that's all there is to it."

I said, "Cheri, that's not true. You are not really that kind of a girl; but you will become that kind of a girl if you continue to see yourself in that way and invite others to see you that way." Then we spent some time talking about love targets, about what we relate to in other people and in ourselves. It was very difficult for her to understand. Finally she broke off our conversation. "It's no good. I'm the way I am, and I can't change. It's very upsetting to me, but there's nothing I can do about it."

What Cheri meant was that she had decided to accept her mutation self as her reality. In her circumstances and situation she had changed until her vision of her own purpose and worth as a beautiful heavenly being had nearly disappeared. She had decided to accept the meager nourishment she had been able to find and to change her identity to make that nourishment satisfactory.

And this is exactly what she finally did; she married a man whom later she described to me as being "the best I could get." I asked her then if she and her husband loved each other. She smiled, hesitantly, and then said, "We take care of each other—that's all love is, isn't it?"

There was nothing I could say. She didn't want help. I felt sad, for here was a beautiful being who had become so blunted in her sensitivities and responses that she had lost her sense of the spiritual basis of life.

When the Lord commanded us to love one another as we

love ourselves, he meant more than Cheri's blunt, gross definition of love as the blind servicing of another person's external necessities. The Lord was stating a factual human relationship. We do, in fact, whether we mean to or not, love others as we love ourselves. We relate to others as we relate to ourselves, and they relate so to us. The great challenge of our earth existence is to keep our spiritual point of view, to nourish our real selves with real love supplies so that we may be free from the mutation process caused by the world and by Satan's deception. Then we will be able to love others freely, without guile. This is the "liberty" to which Paul the apostle proclaims each man is called. This is what Paul means when he appeals to each of us to "walk in the Spirit," for so we all ought to walk.

5

Sighting on Right Targets

Man's earthly existence is but a test as to whether he will concentrate his efforts, his mind, his soul upon things which contribute to the comfort and gratification of his physical nature or whether he will make as his life's purpose the acquisition of spiritual qualities. (David O. McKay.)

Mortal life is exceedingly complex. It is not simple. Our relationships with ourselves and with others reach out in countless directions and contain a multitude of targets. But our primary target, our dominant quest, in all our seeking and relating should always be spiritual, to reach out and touch the heavenly being that dwells within. All other targets, in all areas and to any purpose, must be recognized for what they are and kept secondary to this true primary target.

Some young people exclaim, "We fell in love at first sight. There was no need to consider anything at all. We were just made for each other." What they don't realize, in their inexperience, is that "love at first sight" is usually merely an announcement of a symbiotic relationship, a relationship in which two people find that their external love targets, in this case their unmet psychological needs, match up.

40

For instance, when a 70 percent submissive woman falls in love with a 70 percent domineering man, a symbiotic relationship occurs. Each partner is dependent upon the other partner's mutated love supply to nourish his own mutated need. The woman needs someone to boss her around, and the man needs someone to boss. They don't really *love* each other, but they do *need* each other. Their love targets match up. And because they need each other so desperately, it seems good to them to find themselves so emotionally relieved, even momentarily. It is easy for them to mistake that strong feeling of relief for love; but it is not love, at least the symbiotic part of their relationship is not love. Their feelings of satisfaction and comfort are mostly based upon secondary targets, and their motivations are essentially selfish. Symbiotic love relationships seldom provide the genuine emotional nourishment each partner really needs. Whenever I hear of such a symbiotic relationship, I am reminded of the young girl who was married in such a union; just after she was married, she came to her mother and said happily, "Oh, Mother, I have come to the end of all my problems." Her mother, wiser in her years than her daughter, said, "I know, honey, but you don't know which end."

Our greatest need is to assess and rank our love targets so that we understand *how* we are relating to ourselves and to others. I once read a study done among college men that dealt with the assessment of love targets. Among other questions asked of these young men was this one: "Why do you love your girl friend?" Among the group that later proved very insecure and emotionally unhappy, the answers to this question were inevitably based in external values: "She's a great hostess." "She's a really popular homecoming queen." "Why, she cooks and sews like nobody's business." "If you could see her in a bikini, you'd understand." "She's the only girl who can beat me at tennis." "Mary has a 3.8 GPA." "Her father makes a million dollars a year."

Among the group that later proved emotionally stable and more secure, the answers were based on internal values, upon character traits: "She is gentle and kind." "She is reliable." "She is utterly honest." "She has a great inward beauty." "She's very comfortable to be with."

A second question was equally revealing: "If your girl friend were in an automobile accident and her face were scarred and she were crippled and forced to be in a wheelchair for the rest of her life, would you still love her and stay with her?" The majority of the men in the healthy group replied that they would still love her—indeed, that they would always love her. Their love for their sweetheart was based upon values beyond the condition of her body. But the men in the less stable group said almost unitedly, "No, I would not love her. I couldn't stay with a vegetable." Their love targets were externals. They related to their sweethearts in terms of gain to themselves. Their love was selfish and exploitive. It was mostly ignorant of the real self, the powerful, beautiful, heavenly being that dwelt within the body of the woman they thought they loved.

It is surprising when we consider how many of our love targets are external. We relate to performances, to appearances, to grades, to looks, to money, to sex, to whatever brings a return to us. Our mutated selves are world selves; they are selfish and sensual. They are concerned with surfaces, with society, and with the flesh. They are mutations that receive strength from false nutrients gained from substitute sources. The man who came into my office threatening to divorce his wife because she weighed 247 pounds was openly proclaiming that his love targets in his relationship with his wife were purely physical. He openly stated, "That is not the body that I contracted for." In his marriage he related primarily to his wife's flesh and what that could do for him. He had married a body, not a person. He had no sensitivity to nor even awareness of her spiritual identity, her heavenly being, her real self. This was mutation. And she, perhaps as a consequence, had turned to food as a love substitute for the real nourishment she so vitally needed. This too was mutation. Both of them had become blind to what originally was intended to be.

This sort of reciprocating cycle happens often. It takes

various forms, all mutations of the genuine respect and consideration we ought to have for each other. For instance, tuning a person out, or not listening when a person speaks, is one of these forms. It is prevalent in almost all social relationships, and very prevalent in marriage. As always, it reveals targets and values.

One dissatisfied wife told me that her husband came home every evening, sat down at the dinner table, put the newspaper in front of his face, and began to read and eat. As she tried to talk to him of the things that had happened to her that day, he would nod and murmur between bites of food, "Uh-huh, yes, uh-huh—that's nice, uh-huh, that's fine." He wasn't listening to her, and she knew it deep down inside, but she hated to admit it. "I told myself that I didn't really care," she said, "but then I realized that I did care." She cared because her inside self craved truth and honesty. It hated deception and lies.

That evening, as her husband came home and sat down to his dinner and began to read his newspaper, she began to tell him the things that had happened to her that day, and he said, "Uh-huh, ah-hah, uh-huh," never looking up, never noticing, hardly even paying any attention to the food she had prepared for him.

Without changing her voice level, she had said, "Today we went bankrupt and our new car blew up. I found out that I have cancer and will soon die."

And he had replied, "Uh-huh. That's nice. Fine, honey, fine," not listening, not noticing what she had said, nor indeed that she was even there at all.

In my office, she wept as she talked to me. She knew that this incident was a small thing, but she also had begun to realize why it hurt so, and that realization made it hurt even more. Instead of feeling warm waves of love and respect from her marriage partner, she felt used and insulted. She felt that her being there with him didn't matter to him, at least in the way that she wanted it to matter. He had tuned her out.

In fact, she really didn't matter to him *as a person*. That was obvious. Perhaps she never had. Whatever his original love relationship with her had been, it had now changed until what he sought from her was merely external service, as a housekeeper, as a baby sitter, as a cook. There was little soul target left in his relating to her. As a result, their relationship, their marriage, was mutating into something other than what it was meant to be.

A young woman I know had been engaged to an enterprising young art student. When I asked her how things were going for them, she replied that she had broken their engagement. I said, "Why? How could this be?"

She answered slowly, "Well, I began to realize, I guess, that I was not a person to him. I was only a form to be decorated, to be manipulated, to be looked at and played with. His greatest pleasure was to have me with him to show to other people. He never considered *me*, as a real person. I had no value to him beyond my ability to fill his need." She looked away from me. "It hurt to break it off, but I'm glad I did. I could never have spent a whole lifetime married to him. It would have been awful. I would have become something I simply am not." She paused again, and then looked up. "I can do better than that. I know I can. All the time I was going with Bill I just felt that it was wrong somehow. Something inside of me kept nagging at me to face up to it, I guess. And so at last I did."

And it was well that she did, for she later married a man who did love her for her beautiful self, and she has been very happy. She did well to listen to her inside self, which knew what was real and true and best for her, even though her substitute self presented all kinds of excellent reasons for remaining with Bill. In actuality, she sensed that Bill's love targets were misplaced, and that the false nourishment that she received from him would eventually cause her to mutate and become something other than what she really was. It was a true feeling, a decision from her inside heavenly being, and her behavior in breaking off the relationship matched her true identity. It was a loving act, both to herself and to Bill, whether he realized it or not.

But a person's runners do not all reach out in one direction.

We grope outward for our love supplies in all directions, seeking nourishment from all possible available sources. It's surprising how indiscriminate we can be.

I'll never forget the older man who came in to see me, seriously asking why, when there was so much variety in all the "other sports in the world," was it not permissible for him, socially and ethically, to have variety in sex. I said to him, "Jack, sex is not a sport. It is simply not some kind of international recreation."

"But it most certainly is," he replied. "It really is. Haven't you been to the theater lately, or to the movies? Haven't you read any of the novels on the latest best-seller list? Don't you read *Playboy*? Just look at this," and he took a copy of *Playboy* out of his briefcase. "Don't you know about the new morality?" He looked at me and smiled. "But then you're locked up in this office all day long. How would you ever know about all of that."

I wanted to answer, "From sick people like you; that's how I know about it." But I didn't. I encouraged him instead to talk it out. After quite a long time, he finally unwound and slowed down, and I said to him, "Jack, do you have any children?"

The lights came on in his eyes. "Oh yes, I have children," he said, and he pulled out his wallet to show me pictures of his children. "Here is Helen, and here is Julie, and Kathy, and Bill, and little Harold."

I said to him, "Jack, don't you ever get tired of these same old kids, day in and day out, month after month? Why don't you trade them in and get some variety?"

He looked at me as though he thought I was out of my mind. He began to stuff the pictures back into his wallet. He hadn't liked what I had said. "Oh, no," he said, "I'd never trade in any of these kids. I love these kids." The tears came to his eyes. Then he went on to tell me a story about a lady he knew who had a rich friend who wanted to buy one of her eight children. The lady was poor and needed the money very badly. The rich person had seriously offered her five thousand dollars for any one of her children. That night, she went around from bed to bed, looking at each child, trying to decide which one she would sell. As Jack told me this story, the tears ran down his cheeks, and he had to wipe his face with his handkerchief. It was emotional for him because he really did love his children. Finally, he said that the poor lady decided she couldn't part with any one of her eight children, even for five thousand dollars. And he added, "That's how I love my children. I couldn't stand to part with any one of them."

I said to him, "Jack, why don't you love your wife as you love those kids? You've got one form of love for your children and an entirely different form of love for your wife. Why don't you love Brenda as you love your children?"

That was a new idea to him. He became very defensive. He began pointing out all the ways in which Brenda didn't satisfy him.

"But your children satisfy you," I said.

"Well, I'm not having sex with my kids!" he shouted at me. "And that's the difference."

And that *was* the difference. His love target for his children was completely different from his love target for his wife. He didn't relate to his children as sex objects as he did to his wife. His relationships with his children were based more upon internal values, and therefore that relationship was satisfying to him. But externals ruled his relationship with his wife, and in that relationship, he was miserable and frustrated, groping indiscriminately for every possible new substitute to nourish his misshapen, mutated self.

What he needed to do was assess and order his love definitions. With his children, his definitions were more real and valid. They were more internal and primary. His feelings for them were sensitive and sweet. He cried with the power of them. Because they were congruent with his real self, they satisfied his soul and fulfilled his needs. But in his relationship with his wife he had allowed a secondary target, sex, to become the primary one. The kind of love supply that he sought in her (and other new sources) was a false substitute. It was external and selfish. It was counterfeit. It did not match his true identity nor hers, and was therefore unsatisfactory and miserable.

Variety and novelty used as love substitutes can show how very barren and empty and frustrated the user really is. The misery, loss, and dissatisfaction that follow are inevitable and always accompany counterfeit love supplies from any substitute source. Each man's deep spiritual hunger for purpose and meaning can only be nourished by honest and real love supplies from proper and right sources.

All of our relationships with others and with ourselves are exchanges in which nourishment is given and taken. These relationships should constantly be evaluated in terms of targets (*what* we are aiming for) and motivations (our values, *why* we seek what we seek). Both target and motivation are equally important. Healthy, whole people relate to primary love targets for right reasons. They relate to another person for himself, and not for what he can provide. Sick people relate to secondary targets for selfish fulfillment. They seek gain at the expense of some other person.

When secondary targets based on external values usurp the places of primary targets based on internal values, conditional love supplies are produced. Conditional love is love that is delivered by one person to another upon certain conditions. A person who loses contact with his inside self and loses the vision of his own intrinsic value and purpose goes outside himself to find substitute conditions of worth. When he does this he usually ends up buying love. A purchased love supply is always external and always conditional, for it is delivered upon the payment of price. When we buy our food or clothing or other supplies, our purchases are based on the assumption that we cannot obtain them free. It is so also with our love supplies. When one buys love, he does so with the conviction that love is not freely available to him. Love-starved people lie, boast, and cheat to purchase love because they have found that love does not come to them free, as it ought because they *are* themselves and *are* intrinsically lovable and capable. Their layers and defenses, and the world's barriers and preventions, have caused them to accept and even seek counterfeit nourishment. Purchasing conditional love supplies becomes one of their primary targets. Buying love becomes a measure of personal worth.

It is easy to be caught up in such unhealthy patterns. The world and selfish, unthinking people push them upon each of us. "If you wet the bed, we won't love you anymore." "Grandmother only loves a quiet child." "Go away. Thumbsuckers aren't wanted around here." "We won't like you if you won't let us use your wagon." "If you really meant what you say, you'd take me to the movies." And so on and on. The condition for receiving love is always some performance or appearance according to the demand of the person or group proffering the love supply, and the targets selected or offered are always external, always secondary to the real self and its primary needs.

But more than this, such conditional love retroacts. The "worth" gained, the "love" obtained, not only mutates the user, but also reinforces the false target that is causing the mutation. The reward received from the interaction, when accepted and used, nourishes its own source, thus making the source even stronger. It is a diabolical cycle. For instance, the mother who wanted to hug her son before he went to school (to prove that she was a good mother) was actually attempting to set up such a source. She sought not to give her son support out of her inside self, but to suck nourishment from him to fill her own mutated need. Her hug took; it did not give. It was a substitute and a fake. Nevertheless, her need was so great that she was willing to accept mere form for actuality. Had her son gone through with the form, accepting her acted-out performance, enduring her false affection, she would have derived a kind of nourishment therefrom—but that nourishment would have been counterfeit. It would have nourished only her mutated world self in its already unreal position. Her beautiful, hungering, inside self would have remained unfed and even weakened.

Her son's refusal to participate in this relationship, though probably defensive and revengeful, was nevertheless a good position to have taken, both for himself and for his mother.

The next step would have been to explain and guide the mother to understand her incorrect objective and motivation. In time, with loving patience and persistence, the mother's sincere needs might have been filled in honest and real ways, and her relationship with her son would have changed to what it ought to have been all along.

I talked not long ago with a man who had been in prison for seventeen years. I said to him, "How long has it been since your parents came to see you?"

He said, "Seventeen years."

"How come?"

He looked away but at last replied, "When I came in here, they disowned me. I am no son of theirs, they said, and will never be again." His chin quivered, and his eyes filled with tears. "They said I was no longer worthy to be their son."

How sad—a crime committed, hurt feelings, offended love, and now an even greater crime being perpetuated. The target of his parents' love was their son's performance. It was an external target, and the love supply that they offered to him was conditional and secondary. They could not get beyond his socially unacceptable performance to that precious, real, heavenly being that was his inside self—cluttered, muddled, perverted, and nearly destroyed though it may have been. And so they tuned him out, shut him off, refused to allow him any value as a person. In the process, they nourished in themselves the very mutations that they could not accept in him.

Externals, seen most often in performance and appearance, unfortunately rule most relationship targets. "Oh, I love your long black hair," the young man says to his sweetheart. "If you ever cut it, I'm not sure I could love you as I do." And his statement of love sounds beautiful and flattering, but in reality he is saying, "I don't love *you* at all; it is your long black hair and the excitement it gives *me* that I love." The girl who says to the football hero, "I love you in your uniform; I love to watch you play football," is really saying, "I love your uniform, and I love the game of football." These are all external love targets, and the love supply that they produce is secondary.

Secondary love is not bad in its place, but it must never be allowed to take the place of primary love. Primary love is a love for the spirit self. It takes the form of respect, trust, confidence, and faithfulness toward oneself and toward others. It is completely honest. It presents no conditions except the condition of availability—the more the self grows, uncluttered and free, the more it is available.

There is nothing wrong with the boy's loving his girl friend's long hair. If her hair is truly beautiful, he *should* appreciate it and recognize its impact upon him, but those facts ought not come before his love and appreciation for her inside soul and her feelings. If she cuts off her hair, he should still love her beautiful self. It's the same for the girl who loves the excitement of watching her boy friend playing football. These aspects of their relationship are valid and they can be nourishing, but they must be recognized for what they are and kept in their proper places. It is normal and healthy to appreciate and receive love support from a wife's beauty, or a husband's good providing, or a child's good grades; but one must be sure to keep these separate from his love for the person's inside self, which far outshines all outward forms.

Each person, as a person, merits love and respect, confidence, trust, freedom, faith, purpose, and worth, simply because he *is*. These are his by right of his identity. True love matches the identity of the inside soul of both giver and receiver. It is always a giving or sharing relationship. Its motivation is never selfish.

I recall a young woman whom I had tried to help by friendship and counseling. She came into my office one day and said, "It's very difficult for me to find a place to study during this hour. May I come in your office and study here? I have a class at one o'clock, and your office is close to my classroom. I won't disturb you, I promise." When I said I couldn't allow that, she became offended. "Why can't I study in your office? I wouldn't bother you. If you really loved me as you say you do, you would let me do that."

When I again said that I couldn't have her there, even if she were quiet, she became angry and then defensive. "You don't like me anyway," she said. "You know all about me, and I'm no good." Her lip curled. "I'm not your kind of person. My 'favorite love supply,' as you call it, is sex, and you don't approve of that; you're too straight." She began to cry. "And besides, if you really loved me, I would be your only patient. You wouldn't even see any of these other people."

I said to her, "Shirley, believe me, none of your definitions of love are real. Permissiveness is not love. Sex is not love. That possessive, exclusive relationship in which you would be my only counselee is not love. I would be untrue to myself and untrue to you if I provided you with any of those sick forms of love. Your motivations are wrong and your targets are mixed up."

She didn't like that at all. She gathered up her books and slammed out of the room.

It was almost a year before I saw her again. One morning she came into my office smiling and said that she was sorry that she had been upset the last time she had seen me. She wanted me to know that she was sure now that I had been right all along.

"I'm glad you were firm with me," she said, "and told me what love really is, or maybe isn't. I have been to other therapists since then, and one even took me to bed, but I knew even while that was happening that what we were doing wouldn't satisfy my real needs. I know now that that will never help me feel better about myself."

I have often wondered what became of Shirley. She had a long way to come, but she was beginning to perceive what real love supplies might be. She was beginning to see a small glimmer of true light through layers and layers of mutated self. Her definitions of love were changing, as were her definitions of her exaggerated need for love from others. I remember her saying once, "I need one thousand times more love supplies than anyone alone could ever give." But now her old definitions were proving false. They were inadequate to satisfy her deep spiritual need. For her, things had never been in their right order. Her inside self had never been in control. For her, things had merely happened. There seemed to be no direction, no purpose, no wrong or right. Life was a heavy, blunt, miserable existence—and yet she sensed deep down inside herself that something beautiful and satisfying was missing. She longed for something more soul satisfying than the cheap substitutes she was enduring. At last she had begun to see that her motivations were based upon deficiency, not adequacy, and that her relating targets, even when reached, were not able to satisfy her emptiness and longing.

This is the kind of insight needed to achieve change. It is the kind of insight that produces intelligent repentance. Repentance is always change, and change is growth, or ought to be.

We do grow the way we choose. Our success or failure, our happiness or misery, both now and eternally, depend not only upon *what* we choose to seek after, but also *why* and *how* we choose to achieve it. To make right choices, we need to be sensitive, aware of the ways we reach out for nourishment to our souls. We need to assess and evaluate constantly our motivations and our relating targets, and they must become congruent with the eternal purpose and meaning of our spirit being.

Man has the power within himself to break through the earth's muffling layers that bind and blind him. He is meant to be as the gods, knowing good from evil. He is created in the very shape and image of God, like him in form and manner and future. Our Heavenly Father is the real father of our spirits, the father of those bright, powerful, heavenly beings that inhabit these earthly bodies. Our earth life is our opportunity to become like our Heavenly Father in every way, attaining the same absolute love and security he has attained.

The gospel is the road map. It tells us what to aim toward and why we should aim toward it. It tells us how to achieve. It states clearly that we must have love to live, and that happiness in this world, and out of it, is based upon how we learn to give and receive this love.

6

Choosing Liberty or Captivity

Men are free according to the flesh; and all things are given them which are expedient unto man. And they are free to choose liberty and eternal life, through the great mediation of all men, or to choose captivity and death, according to the captivity and power of the devil. (2 Nephi 2:27.)

When through the gospel, the spirit in man has so subdued the flesh that he can live without wilful transgression, the Spirit of God unites with his spirit, they become congenial companions, and the mind and will of the Creator is thus transmitted to the creature. (Brigham Young.)

No man escapes completely the influence and impact of earth life upon him. Mortality always teaches. Even Jesus knew offense and anger. Even he felt love and loyalty, respect and affection. Assurance and purpose, coming from his spiritual identity, were fruits of his spirit in this mortal existence, even as they are to each one of us. "This is my beloved Son," said his Father to him, again and again, adding encouragingly, "in whom I am well pleased."

How very important it is for us, too, to know our real identity and to be encouraged in our becoming. Repentance and change are laws of life, especially in this life of opposites, of good and bad, pleasure and pain, joy and sorrow. We came here to earth to grow, to change, to learn by our experience to know good from evil, to discern the real from the substitute, to embrace the true over the counterfeit.

But how powerful are the pressures of this earth, of its dimensions of time and space, of cause and effect, of societies and economics. How deceitful the wiles of Satan, who would lie to us, and lead us to false and counterfeiting nourishment, and teach us to love our mutated, substitute selves in place of that heavenly being within us.

But the consequences of earth life are exacting and very real. The atonement of Jesus Christ is intended to help us with these consequences. Mercifully, it provides a way for every man to be released from the perverting aftermaths of earth-life experience and yet allows him to retain the knowledge and power he has thereby gained. It is a great gift, and it works without fail for each one of us if we choose to follow its author's directions.

That we may do this more intelligently and thereby learn and understand, our Heavenly Father has given us an agency, secured by his power and accomplishment, to freely choose our directions and purposes. He has directed us to use this agency to subdue the earth, to overcome its influences, to master its potentials and its relationships. In short, he has directed us to become truly and independently free.

This is the reason for our lives upon the earth, for our mortality, our second estate. We are here to be tried and in the trying, to learn. This is the keeping of our second estate that will make us free as our Heavenly Father is free. Achieving this great liberty is the opportunity that caused the morning stars to sing together and all the sons of God to shout for joy. Our inside spirit selves desire to accomplish this great achievement more than anything else.

We grow and develop in response to the challenges of our earth life. Pushed by interactions with people and forces, we choose and select our direction, seeking love supplies to meet our needs. As our experience expands, we struggle to define what is happening to us; we try to interpret it, to rationalize it, to make it work for us. Eventually we develop patterns of mortal action that, matching our real spirit selves, are very satisfying. Some of the time, for reasons never entirely clear, we may succumb to Satan and our substitute self takes over. This self is not our spirit self. It is a mutation, a substitute, and everything it does is designed to fill some deficiency in our existence with some kind of illusory fulfillment. The ways in which it does this are its styles, the styles of the substitute self.

A style in and of itself may be good or bad. No one creates a substitute self and picks a consequent style unless it satisfies at least three or four strong, unmet, emotional needs. Styles may be either negative or positive. A negative personality style uses externals for love targets. A positive personality style uses internals for love targets. Positive styles are authentic; they express the inside self, securing it proper nourishment and real love supplies, helping it to grow, to become even more glorious and beautiful and independently free and able. Negative styles are unauthentic; they pervert perspectives, victimizing and enslaving the real self, mutating and changing it until it cannot fulfill its original capabilities, making it unable to achieve the great liberty and potential to which it is originally called.

For example, overeating, or being overweight, is a typical style often adopted by a substitute self. This style is pressed into service to fill substitute needs, needs that have taken the place of the original great requirement for nourishment to the inside soul. It is a strong and common style that is difficult to change because it usually serves to satisfy four or five unmet needs in a person's life. One who wishes to quit overeating must discover how each of these needs is being met by eating. He must recognize each need for what it is: an external target that provides a counterfeit payoff. He will then need to fill all of these wants in a real way or he will continue to meet them in a counterfeit way—either by continued overeating or by some other substitute style. Discovering only one need and filling only that, either in a genuine way or in a substitute way, will

she put on more and more weight, not only as a rebellion against her mother, but also to achieve a payoff of false independence.

4. She compensated for her lack of a love relationship with her mother by seeking further love supplies from her father. Her father really liked good food. She found that when she cooked good food for him—fat foods, pastries, cookies—he gave her appreciation and a kind of love. She found comfort in sitting by him and eating the good food that she cooked for him.

It was no wonder that by the time she was twenty-two years of age she weighed 268 pounds. Her style of overeating had made her overweight, and that state provided substitute compensations to ease at least four of the stresses that were so difficult in her life. Her single need of wanting others to like her could not outweigh the pressure of those four larger needs, which she had learned to satisfy by this style of living.

Therapy helped Peggy to understand these causes—what they were and why they existed—and what their payoffs were to her. It was necessary for her to define as counterfeit these methods of satisfying these causes, and finally to see they were not worth the payoffs they brought to her. Understanding is always crucial to any complete repentance. One must know who and what his enemy is before he can successfully position himself to fight and overcome. It is almost impossible to fight an enemy that one cannot see and does not understand. In Peggy's struggle to satisfy her needs, her greatest sin was not gluttony, not excessive eating, but rather her giving the spirit self's job of worth and respect to a substitute style (in this case overeating). This betrayal not only desecrated her spirit self, but actually weakened it so that it was even more inhibited from growing and developing.

The second step for Peggy was to define a plan of action. Merely identifying an enemy never wins a battle. One has to expose the enemy to himself, and to others if feasible, so that he can catch that enemy and stop him. To do this, one has to use some force and take some risk. He must refuse to let substitutes rule his life, mutating and changing his true identity. Peggy would have to start exposing the work of her enemy as soon as she perceived it. As soon as she began overeating she would need to realize, and even say aloud, "Yes, Peggy girl, what you are doing is handling those four needs, but it's sick. It's not getting any *real* love supply. All you are doing is becoming fatter and more false, which means that you'll lose the very love you seek." After Peggy achieves this conviction and restrains her negative self, she will feel her real spirit self emerging and providing the love supply that she so desperately needs and for which her excessive eating has become the substitute. If she is able to get real love flowing into her life, she will have no use for a cheap substitute. She will stop using food for the love she doesn't have.

Her second stress was fear of her own femininity. She was terrified at being a female. She will need to discover the sources for her fear and to refute their authority. She will need to find new motivations that relate positively to being a woman, and that supply her with pleasant and comfortable feelings. She will need to have some positive female experiences, experiences that are not based on abuse, inferiority, and inadequacy. She will need to perceive worth and value in her being a woman in the world.

Peggy's third and fourth stresses were two sides of the same coin. The one was rebellion against her mother, and the other was conforming to please her father. In reality, she needed to become independent of both her parents. The self-assurance she received from hurting her mother was false in that it was not sustaining, but destroying Peggy. It was not love at all, but hate. The love supply she received from her father, at least in the manner she was achieving it, was conditional and false; it too was destroying the real Peggy much more than it was sustaining her. Peggy needed to realize that the rewards she was receiving from her substitute style (overeating) were illusory and not worth the self-desecrating prices she was paying for them. She needed to set up a plan of action to break out of her old habits.

Actually, both rebellion and conformity are usually dependency patterns. They depend upon somebody else; they seldom act spontaneously or independently. Both styles are responses to someone else's initially doing something; then the person adopting the style either does the opposite or follows along. Both styles are substitutes. They both create an illusion of freedom or acceptance. This kind of rebel and this kind of conformist refuse to listen to their true selves, which seek a true liberty based on intelligent free agency and thoughtful considerate choice. They substitute quick counterfeits instead. Overeating, as a style, slips easily into such styles as rebellion and conformity.

At the university, a young man said to me one day, "All my life I've wanted to major in music, and now I can't."

I said to him, "Why not?"

He replied, "I just found today that my mother wanted me to major in music. Now I can't do it."

How foolish is such rebellion in the name of independence! This young man has lost his freedom. He has given it up. All his mother has to do is say, "I want you to do this," and immediately he is bound to do something else instead. How weak and dependent his style is! His freedom is based upon slavery to another person's decisions. He exercises low intelligence and little free agency. Such a style borders upon mental illness. A healthy person listens to other people and takes their opinions under advisement with his spirit self. He evaluates all opinions, listening carefully to the voice of his own capable spirit that is able to tell him what he should do, then he decides his future course of action. He is spontaneous and independent. He does not simply react—he acts.

Rebellion is often a compensation used to support a person's fear of being easily led or controlled. Both rebels and conformists need to find out why they have come to accept an illusion of freedom in the place of real freedom. Real freedom is based upon understanding and following one's real identity. Once that understanding is achieved, neither rebel nor conformist will need what another person has to offer. Each will be independent of any other person's opinion or need.

It is an immutable law in the universe that whoever makes you angry or sad or threatens you in any way has something that you think you need. It is always so. No one can emotionally affect you unless he has something that you want, or think you want. Often you will be surprised to find out that he does not have what you think he has—that you already have it, or with the help of the Lord could have it inside yourself. You may even find out that you don't really need from that person or thing what you had originally thought you wanted.

Peggy said to me one day, "All my life I have wanted love from my mother. But just today I have begun to realize that she doesn't have it to give. She doesn't love herself; how can she love anybody else?" She looked at me through tears. "My whole concept has changed. I used to think that my mother was selfish and had tons of love that she purposely withheld from me because she hated me so. But now I feel sorry for her. She just doesn't have that love to give, not to me nor to others. That's why she doesn't give it to me. She doesn't have it to give, no matter how much I want it." She paused, then finished sobbing, "For the first time, I can cry for her and not for myself."

People who are angry at their parents need to find out why they are angry. What is it that the parent has that the person wants? Often, what the person wants the parent cannot give. "Well, I want her to accept me as I am," one person says. But the chances are, in many cases, that her mother cannot accept her that way. She is too threatened by her. This is especially true in cases of overweight, or publicly known dishonesty, or immorality, or drug addiction, or alcoholism. There is the chance also that in some ways the mother *does* accept her daughter, but that these ways are not the ways the daughter wants. Suppose the mother sees in the daughter the same things that she hates in herself. Then the daughter must come to understand that, to realize that she cannot expect love where there is threat and hate. She needs to say, as Peggy said to me that day, "My mother has an almost empty love bucket.

Why should I keep trying to drink out of it? There isn't enough of the right kind of thing in it. She doesn't have what I want."

The solution, of course, is to find a new source of real and genuine love. Peggy must find some source, some person, some relationship that does have what her real self demands and not what her substitute self wants. When she establishes this, she won't choose to have anger anymore toward her mother; she will be able to see her mother's good points, and feel sorry for her mother's bad ones. She will be able to give her mother love and understanding instead of anger and rebellion, and her father, service and kindness without conformity and taking. She won't need the old styles of rebellion and conformity any longer. And she will have become free, truly free—free from a captivity of believing lies, a captivity that has been destroying her mortal life and corroding her potential for eternal life.

As it is with Peggy, so it is for us. Each one of us can know our choices and how we are choosing. We have indeed been given "all things . . . which are expedient" to achieve "liberty and eternal life." What a waste when we willfully, or wantonly, or even unawaredly, choose "captivity and death" instead.

7

The Will to Change

And now remember, remember, my brethren, that whosoever perisheth, perisheth unto himself; and whosoever doeth iniquity, doeth it unto himself; for behold, ye are free; ye are permitted to act for yourselves; for behold, God hath given unto you a knowledge and he hath made you free.

He hath given unto you that ye might know good from evil, and he hath given unto you that ye might choose life or death; and ye can do good and be restored unto that which is good, or have that which is good restored unto you; or ye can do evil, and have that which is evil restored unto you. (Helaman 14:30-31.)

Most of our substitute-self styles are simply defense systems meant to protect us from being hurt. We have learned by experience that we may be hurt in certain situations, and we have developed a style to protect ourselves. A style is like an iceberg: seven-eighths of the mass of the iceberg is under the water and only one-eighth shows above the surface. Most people are only aware of the surface. They care to see only the outside of things. When change is necessary, they feel that changing the surface is sufficient. But this approach is very hazardous.

Everything in the world has a cause. Human behavior is no exception. The one-eighth of the iceberg that shows itself above the surface of the dark water is but a symptom. It is merely evidence of more. The seven-eighths of the great mass, floating under the water, is cause.

Symptoms are always surface. A person readily acknowledges symptoms because they are usually obvious. He will often admit them openly. He says such things as: "I often study through mealtimes to avoid talking with people." "People make me angry! They're so stupid." "Sure, I like shady jokes—that is, as long as they're not too bad. They always get a laugh." "I don't like to date—but I'll go in groups." "Oh, come on—what's wrong with seeing X-rated movies? They can be really informative." "I only work well alone, but I am so unhappy."

Down below the surface lurks a problem, a real hurt. The person will seldom openly say: "I feel inadequate." "I don't like myself." "I'm afraid of other people." "I use sex for closeness I don't really have." "I get angry because anger keeps people away from me." These realities, though true, are simply too shocking to be admitted even to oneself, and they are much too revealing to be openly proclaimed. Yet, many suffering persons sense them about themselves, and long with all their hearts to change them.

But to really change such outward appearances, we must get to their inward causes. We must dig deeper than just surface. We need to be sensitive to our deeper realities. We need to recognize our love substitutes, understanding not only what yield they bring us, but also what effects they have upon us. Knowledge is power. Ignorance is helplessness. Jesus said, "Ye shall know the truth, and the truth shall make you free." (John 8:32.) If we understand the truth about these things, we will be made free from Satan's lies; we will not be slaves to other people or to our own sins or neuroses. Treating only symptoms is placing a Band-Aid over a cancer. It is foolishness.

There are a few key questions that one might ask himself in order to discover his substitute-self styles, their purposes and origins and yields. These questions must be asked over and over again, and the answers sought at deeper and deeper levels, for many of them are subconscious, locked deep in areas of ignored unawareness.

The first question is: What is my self-concept? In other words, how do I feel about myself? How does it feel to be me? How is it to be Julie, to be Tom? What kind of experience is it to be Shirley? to be Brenda? to be Jack? What are my publicly blossoming symptoms? You may say, "I am shy," or "I am self-conscious," or "I am time-conscious," or "I get upset when people are late." But you must go deeper. For instance, when you become angry, how do you feel about yourself? If anger makes you feel good, why do you feel good? What payoff does your anger bring you? What needs in you does anger satisfy?

The second question is: How do I cope within my self-concept point of view? What styles have I adopted to handle my negative self-concept in various situations? "Well," you may say, "I become shy when I get with a group. I'm afraid that if I talk, others might laugh at me and ridicule me." But what do you actually *do* in such a situation? How do you handle your feeling? Do you withdraw? Are you quiet? When someone asks you a question, do you just sit there, blank? When the person becomes frustrated and leaves you to go to someone else, do you say to yourself, "Good. I'm glad. I avoided risking rejection." And deeper down, do you admit your choice of action and say to yourself, "It worked again"? On the other hand, if a person is sympathetic and kind and says, "I realize how shy you are! I don't want to embarrass you. What can I do for you?" do you say inside of yourself, "Good, he is not laughing at me." And do you realize that your pattern protected you again?

Now your style in both the above situations is the psychological defense you erect to protect your negative self-concept. It is your way of handling that primary lie (that you *are* negative); and it is a lie itself, for it is action that is not congruent with your real self. You have created this second lie to help you adjust to your acceptance of the first lie. Both of these lies come from the father of lies and are meant to clutter and destroy.

It is so with all the styles of our substitute self. If you are often angry in your relationships with other people, you might ask yourself, "How does that anger serve my negative self? Could my anger be my psychological defense? If so, what am I defending? What am I protecting?" Then, if you will seek deeply and honestly, you will probably find that your anger is a defense, a constantly thickening cover around your deep inner hurt that comes from your accepting in the first place that you are not lovable and not capable.

If someone has made you angry, then he has hit a sore spot, no matter what it is. He has struck you in a psychological wound. But it is not his fault that you have a wound. Your wound is part of your negative self. The other person has not created your wound; you made it all by yourself. It is true that you would not hurt had your wound not been struck, but, at the same time, the presence of the wound is your responsibility. Perhaps Terri shouldn't go around saying things like that, things that hurt you, but, at the same time, perhaps you shouldn't be so fragile and vulnerable in that area.

It is a great discovery to find out that you, and only you, are responsible for your feelings. You make your own choices. You even choose your own problems. You are not a victim of somebody else's sins. Your wounds are truly your own. They are part of your negative self-concept. And your styles are how you choose to support and nourish that self-concept, as it is confronted by various situations.

Let us suppose that two young girls are standing in the hallway at the high school. Both of these girls are unattractive by society's standards. They have big noses, buck teeth, braces, pimples, everything that pretty girls are not supposed to have. Now one girl knows, because she has been reared with a spiritual perspective and lots of real love, that her nose does not fit the society mold and that her complexion is undergoing a change. She is aware that *Vogue Magazine* and *Seventeen* do not approve of dental braces and do not consider glasses lovely, but she is able to say, "I am a good person, even though my body does not presently fit the society mold. I am a valuable person, and I love myself very much. My body has problems, but it is just a secondary part of the real me." But the other girl has only a worldly perspective and inadequate love supplies. She thinks, because her nose is big and she has glasses and braces and pimples, that she has no worth, that she is not wanted by anyone. "I am not lovable," she says. "I am not capable. I am not beautiful. I am nothing." She believes the world's lies. She accepts her mutated self as her real self. She is becoming what other mutated people have told her she is.

As these two girls stand there in the hall, along comes the captain of the football team. He has a very inflated ego. He feels very aggressive and very falsely and superficially confident. He says, as he goes by, "You girls are really ugly. You are bad news. Why don't you get lost?" And he saunters a few steps down the hall, then looks back. He sees that one of the girls has burst into tears, and he starts to laugh, but the other girl looks him right in the eye and says, "Buddy, *you* have the problem, not I."

Of these two girls, one is very vulnerable. She has a gaping emotional wound. The football captain hit her in her wound and partially destroyed her. But the other girl has a strong self-concept. She thinks of herself as a good person, even though she knows her body doesn't fit some temporary society mold. She is able to say calmly and correctly to the football captain, "*You* have the problem. You must have had a fight with your mother, or something. What are you doing going around at eight-thirty in the morning telling other people that they are bad news? What is the matter with *you*?" Because she is secure in herself, she is not brought down or enslaved by the football captain's sick patterns; she is able to consider the source of what she hears and is able to judge that the boy's position is unreliable and false. Thus, she is able to maintain her freedom and balance. But the other girl is so exposed that she just crashes and cries; her negative self-concept, so crippled and misshapen, cannot handle the situation. She has become dependent upon the boy's view of her for her feelings of worth.

He has something she wants—approval. She is therefore very vulnerable to him.

I had a patient once at Michigan State University who had been at the university for six weeks and in that time had had five different roommates. She said to me, "Every one of those roommates made me so mad that I could hardly stand her. Betty Jean didn't make her bed right. She pulled her spread up and left all the wrinkles underneath. Pam always left the cap off the toothpaste, and toothpaste all over the medicine cabinet. Jody never knew what was going on. The minute she came into the apartment, she started asking the same questions over and over again. I simply couldn't stand it." On and on she went. Finally she said, "You know, I shouldn't get so angry at such little things, but it's so hard." A few weeks later she was talking again about these things that made her so angry. And she said, "You can kill a bird with a BB."

I looked at her, surprised. It didn't seem to make sense. I said, "You're not flipping out on me, are you, Karen?"

"No," she replied, "but I wish I were an elephant."

When I raised my eyebrows at that, she said, "Well, I do. An elephant has a thick skin. You can shoot a BB at an elephant and it wouldn't even bother him. He wouldn't even turn around. He wouldn't care about a little BB. He's so big and strong. I wish I were an elephant and had that thick skin, but I'm just a little bird—and when you shoot a BB at a little bird, you kill it."

Karen saw herself as a nothing. She was helpless and vulnerable; the only way she had found to defend herself was to attack. Her substitute style was anger; she defended her negative self by attacking others because she felt so vulnerable.

The third question one should ask himself in order to discover his styles is historical. It requires digging into the past. It asks, "How did my self-concept get the way it is? What are the threatening hurts it defends me against?"

Some of us resent these kinds of questions. We don't like going beneath the surface, pulling back the cover, digging through our layers and into our garbage piles. We don't like pushing aside the bark mulch and laying back the black plastic. We feel exposed. We feel fear. We don't want anyone to see our layers. We don't even want to see them ourselves. But this too is a defense, for one must always go back into the past to understand the present.

I often ask those who are reticent and afraid to talk of these things to write out their feelings instead. Although keeping a daily journal is not as therapeutic as discussing with a healthy companion, it can be a good beginning. But one must write more than mere events. He must think and react. A faithfully kept journal can become a great help, a trusted listener with whom one shares his deepest feelings and most profound observations about his life and world, their beauty and ugliness. Keeping a journal can be a healthy and insight-producing experience because it not only helps a person think about what is happening to him, but it also helps him take a position and express his feelings in words.

Unfortunately there are some who turn even this potentially powerful and useful cathartic exchange into a substitute style. They learn to enjoy the process. It becomes a kind of a sick game. They strip the plastic back and begin to examine each rambling, pale, misshapen root. They go back over and over the layers, relishing each piece of clutter. "Oh, what does this look like now?" they say. "I wonder how long this has been there." They go through therapy for years, going over each piece of garbage again and again. "Oh, my mother put this one here," they say, or "My father put that one there." I say to them, "You talked about that one last week, Shirley." And Shirley replies, "But I want to talk about it again." These kinds of people don't really want to get well, but they do want to go through the motions of getting well. They don't want to leave therapy because they're afraid they won't find any other love supplies equal to what they are receiving there. Usually they are afraid to cross over and trust their real self. They fear there isn't any real self, so they stay in the negative. Therapy itself has become for them a substitute style.

It's not healthy to spend every day looking at your garbage pile and wallowing in it. Having seen what happened in the past, one should begin to see what must happen in the future. For instance, some people continuously blame their parents and others for all their problems. When they do this, they are implying that they themselves never made any contribution to these problems, but this is not true. Others might have been responsible in the beginning for encouraging or even creating terrible problems, but they are not responsible for finishing them or keeping them now. Each person is in charge of that himself. If it were any other way, we would be helpless to undo it. We would not be able to repent or to progress without some other person's doing something first. We would not be free; we would be trapped and helpless.

Handling life's problems is every man's own opportunity. Everyone must learn to recognize his problems and then set up a plan of action for coping with them. He must say, "I don't have to be this way all my life. I *can* change. I don't have to continue to see things the way I have seen them. I don't have to believe that my garbage pile is me. There is a deeper center to me, a beautiful, ageless self from another dimension. I want to uncover that heavenly being and nourish it, so it can do its work, so that I can be happy and secure."

Digging into the defensive layers, though often uncomfortable, is absolutely necessary. But it must be done intelligently and with care in an atmosphere of love and safety, and with a good guide. The great need is for us to identify ourselves *and* our opposition. We have to understand how and why our substitute styles have developed before we can change them.

The choice must be to return the real self to power, no matter how painful the process. The beauty that awaits us in overcoming the deceptions of our mortality is indescribable; we long in our heavenly beings to maintain our first estate and to become independently free and able as our heavenly parents have become.

We were not meant to fail.

8

Filling the Empty Places

*They are the very handcuffs, and chains, and shackles, and
fetters of hell. (D&C 123:8.)*

Any personality style, supportive to our spiritual identity or
not, can be detected by the way a person handles stress. There
are many kinds of stress, but all eventually come back to
whether or not a person is being treated with the kind of love,
or respect, needed to match his spiritual identity. Love deprivation is Satan's most powerful tool. With it, he manipu-
lates men into positions wherein they choose to frustrate their
own progress in this life—and thereby inhibit their eternal
progress.

For instance, mental illness (or loss of emotional well-
being) is a reaction to stress. It is a concentration of substitute-
self styles that interact with one another. Mental illness is a
way of handling deprivation, a way of getting substitute love
when one does not have an adequate real love supply. Because
mental illness is a counterfeit, it is inevitably destructive, for as
the mentally ill person mutates to meet the counterfeit love
supply, his mental illness style itself becomes a second stress to

be satisfied by further substituting, and further mutation, and so on and on. It is circular—it feeds on itself. Encouraging substitute styles is the work of the devil, and the styles themselves, whether major or minor, extreme or moderate, are "the very handcuffs, and chains, and shackles, and fetters of hell."

None of us escapes having experience with substitute styles. The world is too much with us. Recognizing our own substitute styles can help us understand ourselves so that we may intelligently maintain our first estate. But we must remember that classifying substitute styles provides only a means to discuss and examine; it does not provide cures. Discerning the sources of our love substitutes does not always reveal how we may change these sources. Change is up to each of us alone. Repentance of any kind is always personal. However, putting labels on kinds of behavior can be very helpful, depending upon our spiritual and emotional maturity, our purpose, and our desire.

In order to perceive categories, we sometimes talk in extremes. Extremes help us see patterns and their payoffs, their yields, their results. Always, in extreme cases, people have intense emotional stress. They endure great deprivation, great deficiencies in love supply. Always, in time, they cast about seeking some kind of relief. Such persons usually have people around them whom they copy, models who are themselves using extreme styles to fill extreme unmet needs.

One very prominent type of substitute-self styles is called *psychosis*. The psychotic person handles stress by escaping. He makes a massive change in his reality, adopting a whole new dimension of things. He creates a fantasy situation that puts him grossly out of contact with what really is. He does this to escape from pain. In time, he becomes addicted to his fantasy life; his fantasy protects him from hurt, from the agony of his deprivation. His fantasy life gives him substitute love supplies in place of those genuine supplies he does not find in real life.

And the style works, somewhat adequately anyway. Extreme psychotic people tend to lose their anxiety. They will rarely have ulcers, colitis, nervousness, stuttering. Their fantasy worlds are so massively powerful, so mutating to their real selves, that anxiety is rare. But their fantasy style shuts off their sensitivities and their awareness. It closes the doors in their eyes; it turns off the lights in their souls. Psychotic people soon take on a kind of waxy appearance. Their cover thickens over their layers of pain. They retreat inside and cover themselves over so that they don't have to cope with reality. When this style takes over completely, the psychotic person may be sent to an institution, which is, in reality, a kind of temporary giant womb where everything is taken care of for him. He doesn't have to pay his income tax; he doesn't have to meet his bills or obligations; he doesn't have to worry about his children, their bedwetting, their thumbsucking, their crying, their grades in school, their dating, their threats and problems; he doesn't have to worry about his job or his wife; he doesn't really have to worry about anything. Everyone tells him to "be good and be happy," and he gets lots of rest and lots of conditional "love" supplies.

With treatment, psychotic people usually do modify their style. Sixty to seventy percent of the patients in mental hospitals are eventually released. But when they return to their old environment, to the same situations and associations that originally deprived them, the patterns may come back, and often, after several years, many of these people return to the hospital for further "treatment."

It is very easy to commit crimes against society and reality when one has accepted psychotic disorder as a substitute style, because psychotic disorder is a distorted perspective. It insists upon changing reality to meet a personal demand. *Schizophrenia*, a type of psychotic disorder, means *split from reality*. There are many types of schizophrenia. One often-seen pattern is *paranoia*, wherein a person accepts a fantasy of persecution and adopts a defensive style of being very suspicious of other people. He feels certain of continued rejection and so he creates a fantasy world of suspicion in which it is permissible for him to fight against the hate and antagonism that he is sure is around him.

I worked for a while with a prisoner who had adopted a paranoid schizophrenic style. He was in the penitentiary for murder. He told me that a little eight-inch man told him what to do—whom to shoot, who was out to get him, and how he could best protect himself. The prisoner told me, "When I'm all alone and feel like a failure, and that I'm no good and that nobody cares about me—not even my girl friend comes to visit me in prison anymore—this little man appears, and he comes right up on the table. I can't see his face—I can't catch him." He swung his arm out in a quick gesture. "I've tried to catch him, but I can't. But he's right there, and he stands right there on the table and talks to me. He's my friend. He really is." He lowered his voice. "This little man tells me who to watch out for. He warned me once that a guard was after me and was going to kill me—but I was able to kill that guard before he could get to me. I know it sounds crazy," and he began to cry, "and sometimes I think I'm losing my mind, but I *do* see this little man, honest I do. He really *is* there. I see him and he talks to me. He understands me. He tells me that I'm all right, and I feel good after I talk to him. I feel good after I do what he tells me to do."

This prisoner's thinking was grossly distorted. He was out of contact with reality, but his fantasy was very real to him. It was his way of coping with stress, with pressure, with a deprivation of a love supply that he needed so strongly that he was willing to kill to compensate for it. Paranoia was his substitute-self style; it was his mutation-self pattern of defense and escape.

His situation, though extreme, is typical of what happens in many of us when we do not have the emotional support we so deeply require. Our substitute selves are powerful enough to devise ways to satisfy our unmet love needs, ways that range from character disorders, hallucinations, and fantasies, down to common, everyday styles such as publicly playing the martyr or privately thinking "poor me," or being shy, or always being right, or showing false superiority in numerous ways. Clearly, the prisoner's little man was fashioned to fill his unmet love needs—the little man came to him when the prisoner was at his lowest ebb in love supplies, and the little man comforted him and reassured him, and gave him advice and confidence. He brought the prisoner substitute love supplies, love supplies that were not real, that were counterfeit, that were lies. And the relief they created was temporary and unreal. The prisoner even sensed that they were an illusion, but he was willing to take them because, sadly enough, they were all he had.

Another major substitute style is called *neurosis*. A neurotic person is also out of touch with reality, but he is not so grossly out of touch. Neurotic styles may be adopted even while the original situation is still happening, or they may be adopted consequent to the original happening. There may be phobic reactions, wherein one transfers from one object to another some compulsive fear associated with the original threatening situation. The association may be exceedingly remote. For instance, I know a man who paints for a living. He tells me he has always been afraid of heights, of mountains and mountain climbing, and of flying in airplanes. But lately this fear of heights has been transferred to climbing ladders. He is afraid he may fall. It has come finally to a point where he has a phobia— a fear of all ladders. He has had to hire other painters to paint above doors because he fears falling from a ladder. He is not yet sure exactly what the source of this phobic reaction is, but through finding it and understanding it, he will be better able to cope with it than he is at present.

I recall a very insecure older woman who, as a little girl, stood on a bridge over a railroad track. In those days, steam engines pulled the trains. One day as a steam engine went under the bridge, it blew its whistle. The steam from the whistle scalded the little girl's bare legs. The burns were painful to her, and her recovery from the experience, the pain, and the fear was long and difficult. But though her legs recovered, her mind did not. She became afraid of all trains. Gradually this pain-fear transferred to bridges where there were railroad tracks, and finally even to bridges where there were no railroad tracks. She was afraid to stand upon bridges anywhere, and finally afraid to walk across them. Then she was afraid to go out and walk upon the street. Now, in her later years, she stays in the house most of the time because when she stays in, nothing painful happens. With each successful avoidance of pain, her neurosis was reinforced. It has now become her style, her way of avoiding pain.

Neurotic behavior serves to avoid a threatening situation and relieves the stress of that situation. An employer called me one day and asked if I would take time to talk with one of his receptionists. She was a married woman, about thirty-seven years of age, not very attractive, and from a religious background. During the last few months, she had begun to leave her desk frequently to go to the restroom to wash her hands. Her co-workers reported that she was washing her hands as many as thirty-five times during the working day. When I talked with her, I found her easy to talk with, but also afraid of me. When I asked her why she left her desk so often, she replied, "To wash my hands." And when I asked her why she felt she needed to wash her hands so much, she said she needed them to be clean. "Each time I wash my hands," she said, "I feel a little cleaner. I really do." And so we talked, seeking to understand this neurotic obsession; finally we came upon the real stress situation.

She had been extremely lonely in her life. Her husband had tuned her out; sometimes he didn't talk to her for months on end. He would come home after work, read the paper, and go to bed. There was little or no communication. Her children were in school and seldom at home. She was lonely and felt useless. Her sources of love supply, such as they were, were steadily decreasing. As she cast about for new love supplies, she decided she needed to get out of the home. Quite by chance she had secured her present job as a receptionist. She liked her work; her boss was exceedingly kind. Her co-workers were good to her, but she was still lonely. Each night when she returned to her home, she felt a great emptiness inside herself. No one wanted her, she felt. It was overwhelming.

It so happened that at her place of employment, between 11:30 and 1:30, everyone in the office was gone except her. She was there to receive anyone who might come, to answer the telephone, and to take care of any business matters. This also was the time when the man came with the interoffice mail. This mailman often sat and rested there in her office and talked with her. He, too, had an uncomfortable marriage and an unhappy relationship with his wife and his children. In a short time, these two lonely, unhappy people became physically close to each other; soon they were involved in a sexual relationship. Physical love-making became a substitute love supply for them. Almost every day between 11:30 and 1:30, she and the mailman were using sex to satisfy their hunger for love and belonging, trying to fill the great emptiness each felt in his life. The woman could not help feeling guilty about her actions. She felt dirty. She felt unclean. She began washing her hands. That made her feel cleaner. Every time she washed her hands, she felt better (even though she wasn't better), and gradually as this neurotic style worked deeper and deeper into her, she felt an increasing need to wash her hands more often. And, as always, the substitute style worked. The sexual relationship, which was itself a substitute style, paid off in a counterfeit feeling of fulfillment—she was temporarily wanted and desired. And the obsessive, compulsive reaction of washing her hands salved her conscience; it made her feel cleaner. But it was all wrong. Such styles as these were foreign to her real and beautiful self. The feelings of love and fulfillment that she received were cheap and counterfeit. They were false, and therefore destructive to her personality and to her real self, her spirit that dwelt within.

Many of us are involved to some extent in neurotic substitute styles. Many of us at times adopt styles that are a bit out of touch with reality but that help us to avoid discomfort. These may simply be general anxiety reactions, such as nervousness, nervous excitement, even hysteria, or long sieges of crying. The payoff from such styles is relief from the stress of the tension: nervousness and excitement do usually bring help from others; crying does relax us and bring sleep. All of these sorts of styles have some connection with securing love reinforcement, with securing a temporary illusion of solution, an acceptable escape from a situation that is painful. They are styles devised by the substitute self and are usually adopted early in life and carried on, more or less, for years.

Many people find their anxiety decreased when they straighten the newspapers at night, or when they wash all the dishes before they go to sleep. Some people can't sleep at all until the dishes are done or even until the whole house is cleaned. These are compulsive reactions. They are neurotic, but only in a minor way. People so oriented have developed a few neurotic love substitutes. Their clean house means more to them than their sleep. They are somewhat out of touch with reality. But their pattern does make some sense, and usually it produces some temporarily satisfactory results.

Nevertheless, at the bottom of all these substitute styles, major and minor, is a negative self-concept. People with positive self-concepts are not so anxious; they are not so nervous; they are not so easily excitable. They do not have to wash their hands thirty-five times each day in order to feel clean. They do not have to be afraid of high places, or of steam engines, or of water, or of heights. People with positive self-concepts accept themselves for what they really are. Their lives are in congruence with their spiritual identity; they have real purpose and enjoy genuine feelings of worth. They feel adequate. They do not feel the need to devise ways to secure substitute love supplies through strangely disordered patterns of thought and action.

A third large pattern is *psychophysiologic,* or *psychosomatic* disorders. This is where the stress target is the body. Substitute love supplies can be obtained through the body. For instance, by becoming ill, a person may avoid stress and buy love and attention. Through his illness he gets the substitute love supply that he misses in his real life.

Such physical illness is not fake. It is real. People really have ulcers and colitis because they worry so much. It is true that the worry may be caused by fear and by doubts of adequacy to cope with some situation, but the worry and anxiety cause them to hurt their body; their digestion acids do eat holes in their stomach. They actually do develop all sorts of other gastrointestinal reactions. And even though these reactions cause the person pain, even great pain, the style works for them—they get the love supply that they have felt they lacked, or at least they get a substitute for it. It is better to them than nothing. A father said to me, "It is the only way I get any attention in my house—to be sick. My children see then what they are doing to me, and they begin to pay me some attention." A young child said, "I am sick because I do not want to fight Tommy. Tommy has promised he will fight me when I come back to school."

Stress situations are taken care of by these psychosomatic substitute styles. They start in the head and are taken out on the body. But the illness *is* genuine. It is not fake. The negative self here is king, and it can make the body do what it wants it to do.

People usually adopt this kind of style after seeing someone else using it successfully. Most often, someone in their home already has adopted this kind of style. There is a vast variety of psychosomatic styles to select from, all the way from body aches and pains, migraine headaches and fainting spells, through momentary blindness, humming in the ears, sexual frigidity and impotency, to asthmatic and arthritic conditions. These are genuine hurts. They are genuinely painful. It is wrong to say to people who have adopted psychosomatic styles, "There is nothing wrong with you. It is all in your head." This may have been true originally, but now the pain is real. It is genuine pain, and the suffering can be intense.

The biggest problem with these styles is that they are so difficult to give up. People don't want to give them up, even though they are painful to them, because the physical pain seems little compared to the vast emotional emptiness that the physical pain is filling. But these styles can be changed. People who adopt them need genuine love supplies—and they need to learn how to receive these. They need to understand the substitute style that they have adopted, and they need to convince themselves that they should give up this style, just as they previously convinced themselves to adopt it.

Another major substitute style often seen is called *personality* and *character disorder*. The target here is people. Those who adopt this style seek to hurt themselves and others in order to protect themselves. They will abuse themselves and other people in order to escape or revenge the stress of their anxiety. There are several major patterns or social reactions within this style. Among these, passive-aggressive actions, active-aggressive actions, and sociopathic actions will serve as clarifying examples.

The passive-aggressive person asserts himself by being passive. He tries to make other people angry by doing nothing or by being silent. I have heard wives say, "I would rather, a hundred times, have my husband yell and scream and fight with me, than just be silent while I suffer." When a husband does this, refusing to discuss, he is using passive aggression. This is the silent treatment. A little child who sits at the table and refuses to eat and to talk is being passively aggressive. It is a very effective style. The mother becomes exasperated and finally says angrily, "You will *not* get down from the table until you eat those peas." And the little child just sits there and stares at his plate. The angrier and more frustrated the mother gets, the more the child passively asserts himself. He just remains silent, and finally falls asleep with his head right down in the peas. What can the mother do? She says to herself, "I can't leave him there all night." And so she lifts him down from the chair, carries him up to his bed, and tucks him in, and the little boy wins the battle—with passive aggression.

Active aggression is where there is active violence. People who adopt this style assert themselves by physically or verbally attacking others, by shouting at them, by hitting them, by beating them up. Their personalities have mutated to the point that they mistake for love the forced attention and allegiance that comes to them from such actions. A father who receives absolute obedience from his children by frequent physical punishment, who says, "I will whip him—he will *not* do that anymore," is using active aggression. The father feels secure in his position of father as long as he is physically able to dominate his loved ones and force his will upon those who are dependent upon him.

Sociopathic reaction (which used to be called psychopathic personality) means that a person's capability to receive or give any love supplies at all has perished. Such a person has never had any love supplies. He is empty. When he was born, he received no love at all; no one cared about him. He was used selfishly and meanly by his parents and others. His character and personality have so mutated that he no longer seeks for love. He doesn't care about feeling. He doesn't even know what love is. He has become hardened. He has mutated to the point where he is not able to feel anyone else's feelings. He is insensitive to other people's needs or hopes and to the beauty of things. Tenderness, kindness, appreciation, parenthood, children—indeed, all the sweet things of life—are not within his experience or knowledge. These are the people who become hardened criminals. They would as soon kill a person as steal his pocketbook. There is no difference to them between these two actions. The sociopathic style is a total mutation where the inner spirit self is completely stifled and never allowed at all to emerge in any way or form.

Experience has proven that rehabilitation accomplishes little for a sociopathic person. He just doesn't care. He has no feeling or sensitivity. He does not believe in love. He has learned to assert himself by hurting himself and by hurting others. Drug addiction, prostitution, sexual deviation, assault, rape, murder, all kinds of abuse and use of other people for selfish gain are sociopathic styles. The man who came to me insisting that sex was a new form of personal recreation was tending toward this kind of behavior. Sex, to him, was void of feeling, preciousness, permanency, or dedication. The contrast between his "love" for his wife and his present "love" for his children was the contrast between two styles; but as his children matured sexually, his style of loving them as children could change, and abuse, even incest, might possibly result. Shirley, who wanted to study in my office and who felt that her favorite love supply was sex, was bordering upon the sociopathic. Her "needs" were so exaggerated that she was willing to destroy another woman's family, to destroy another woman's marriage, to even destroy the security of little children to momentarily satisfy herself. She did not care about others' feelings. She was insensitive to the beauty of married love, to the sacred power of the sexual union. She was insensitive to the beauty and preciousness of these things rightly used. When I tried to explain them to her and told her that her body in its potential was powerful and beautiful, like a great cathedral, she said flatly, "I am no cathedral."

"Shirley," I said, "you are burning your cathedral to fry an egg."

But she could not understand. And the insensitive therapist who took her to bed to please himself was just as sociopathic as she was, using her even as she was using him.

One last category of popular substitute-self styles is often called *transient situational personality disorder*. This is a kind of catch-all category that contains many minor forms of the patterns already discussed. These are transient adjustment reactions. They are the styles by which some people tentatively adjust to temporary traumatic situations. They are not chronic patterns. They can be seen clearly in three areas: childhood adjustment reactions, adolescent adjustment reactions, and adult adjustment reactions.

An adjustment reaction is what one does when faced with a momentary stress situation. It may be a one-time-only occurrence, a one-time-only reaction.

A young boy faced with the agony of having to sell his dog may, for instance, run away from home. This is his childhood adjustment reaction to this single powerful situation. A child who goes through a time of being late to school because he does not like his teacher is acting out a childhood adjustment reaction. A child who becomes ill one morning because he is afraid of the youth at school who intends to beat him up that day is adjusting to a childhood stress situation.

The teenage boy who breaks up with his long-time girl friend and goes out and gets drunk is probably merely acting out an adolescent adjustment reaction. Young people who begin to drink, or to use drugs, or to experiment with sex, may begin these styles as transient situation personality disorders. These styles often begin as adolescent adjustment reactions. The problem is that these patterns may become chronic, and sometimes totally destructive.

Some marital problems and some divorces may be adult adjustment reactions. The couple who quarrel over their plans for a summer vacation or who often have words over whether a child should be allowed to go to the movies or not are living through adult adjustment reactions. These kinds of substitute styles are usually temporary. Even though such situations may last from several weeks to a year or two, the persons involved usually return to their more permanent patterns as soon as the transient situation has resolved itself.

These five general categories of "disorders" are really substitute styles that people adopt variously to handle stress. They are ways to fill with something else the empty places where real love and being ought to be.

9

Men Are That They Might Have Joy

Mind is the master power that molds and makes,
And man is mind, and evermore he takes
The tool of thought, and shaping what he wills,
Brings forth a thousand joys, a thousand ills.
He thinks in secret, and it comes to pass;
Environment is but his looking glass.
                    — James Allen

In actuality, all substitute styles are disorders. Order would be congruency, and would reflect an accurate perspective, a deep knowledge of truth. Were we completely in order, we would be able to see ourselves not only as others see us, but as we really are, and we would act in ways congruent with our true nature. We are assured that such great insight will eventually come to each one of us in the resurrection, but in the meantime we are in this world, and we must understand what is happening to us.

The substitute styles we choose and the love needs they satisfy depend upon what we think of ourselves. Substitute styles always meet our demands. They accurately support, compensate, or cover up the lies we have come to believe about ourselves.

It follows, then, that achieving a more correct concept of who we are must result in a realignment of what we feel to be our needs, and a consequent abandonment of substitute styles that feed and reinforce our errors. The more correct this self-concept is, the more realistic will be our thinking and the more authentic will be our behavior. The truly aware persons needs no substitute styles, no false pay-offs, no counterfeit rewards. His joy is in his being, his glorious heavenly being, and that secure knowledge is so thrilling and so deeply and quietly joyous that he seeks only to share his fullness with others. He has no desire to take, possess, or exploit. What a great contrast this is to the scheming, taking, selfish styles encouraged by Satan and by the world and its deceptive dimensions. Our challenge, then, is to remember who we are and act accordingly, and thereby achieve great joy and eternal happiness.

But the way is not easy. It was not meant to be. We begin to develop substitute styles very early in our lives. By the time we are about eight years of age, most of us have made very definite choices. Some major environmental factors influence what we choose.

The first and primary factor is the availability of real love supplies in our family. If genuine love supplies are available, then the real self confidently emerges and the substitute self is not necessary. The child's style will be authentic and real. If, however, love supplies are much restricted or are substitute and false, the need for substitute styles, to secure substitute nourishment, increases. The more deprived a child is, the more intense becomes his need.

A second factor is the order of the child's birth, both by sex and by years. A baby who closely follows another boy has less chance of successfully copying the older boy's substitute styles. But if a boy follows a girl, there is more chance for his success should he copy his sister's styles. Because sex difference easily provides uniqueness (a substitute for real identity), it is not as threatening for a boy to copy an older sister's styles, or for a girl to copy an older brother's styles, as it is for a sister to copy a sister, or a brother to copy a brother. And because there is rivalry in performing for different audiences, the closer two babies are in years, the less the chance of successful copying; and likewise, the farther apart in years, the more chance there is of copying.

A third factor is the social need to be different. Being different is an external substitute for genuine internal self-assurance. Uniqueness, *per se,* offers a substitute identity that pays off in an illusion of importance and monopoly. If a certain substitute style is taken already by one brother or sister, the child in need will struggle to find a different style in order to establish his own uniqueness. For instance, if an older sister is learning to play the piano and is receiving conditional love and approval that way, the next child may desire to play the clarinet or perhaps the trumpet, or he may choose not to play a musical instrument at all. Depending upon the availability or scarcity of love supplies in his family, plus the depth of his need, he may choose athletics, or scholarship, or some style even more remote from the piano style his sister has already chosen. His choice will reflect his need to be different, his desperate need to guarantee conditional support and approval for himself. This kind of desperate need for some kind of approval, even though conditional, does not exist in the healthy child who is receiving genuine love in support of his real identity. Being alike, especially externally, is no threat or even bother to the loved child. He is adequate in himself, and the consequent healthy joy of being real, of being true to himself, far surpasses any trivial external pay-off from "being different" (or, indeed, for "being the same," as when children, and adults, copy their peers to obtain their love and approval).

The fourth factor is the models the parents allow or prohibit in the child's environment. There are plenty of models and examples available. Parents, brothers, sisters, movie and TV heroes, peers, neighbors, all serve as examples for a child who is searching for a productive substitute style. It has been proven that in families where parents or older children rely on drugs (even legal drugs), the probability of a younger child's also taking drugs is multiplied eight to nine times. Likewise, in homes where parents or older children are active in civic or church groups, the probability of a younger child's also being so active is accordingly increased. But parents and home environments vary. Some parents are very permissive, allowing their children to be exposed to all kinds of models of styles of behavior. Other parents are more restrictive. Some parents make a Grand Central Station of their living room by leaving the TV on all day, allowing a thousand sick models and styles to parade before their children's minds, with little restriction or guidance. On the other hand, other parents are very strict, actively prohibiting the presence of certain models in their home. Regardless, by the time a child is seven or eight years of age, he has made some definite choices as to the substitute styles that are acceptable in his world. These are the styles he will adopt, the ones he has decided will work for him.

Each style a child chooses will be a style that accommodates four or five urgent needs. Each will be rooted in his negative self-concept. A child's self-concept is based mostly on what he thinks his parents and brothers and sisters feel about him. His self-concept may or may not be the truth, but it is always the truth *for him*. If his parents have known their own heavenly identity and have loved and respected themselves for this, so, probably, will their child; he will be authentic and real, even as they are. But if they have not been so, probably neither will be their child, for even as they are, so will he usually be—muffled, stifled, mutated, struggling to find and adopt styles that meet his environment-learned substitute needs and definitions, whatever these may have become.

In all human interactions, three types of performance can be identified. One of these is doing *wrong things for wrong reasons*—action motivated by identity deficiency. When one overreacts, or lies, or shows off, he is doing a wrong thing for a wrong reason. When a person belittles or abuses another person in order to assert himself, he is doing a wrong thing for a wrong reason. The attention he gets in any of these performances is not a real love supply; it is a cheap substitute. The young lady who wore her skirts so short in order to display her well-shaped legs was doing a wrong thing for a wrong reason. The payoff she received, the attention she exacted, was not a real love supply, but a cheap substitute that she had trained herself to accept and even momentarily to enjoy.

Another type of interaction is doing *right things for wrong reasons*. This too is action motivated by love and identity deficiency. The person does do a right thing, but he does it in order to fill his deficiency. For instance, a person who chews his fingernails to allay tension or lack of confidence is doing a wrong thing for a wrong reason. But when he stops this because his parents and others tell him that only babies chew their fingernails, then he is doing the right thing, but for the wrong reason. He has stopped chewing his fingernails, but he has stopped in order to receive a love supply based on a false self-image. He is not more adult for not chewing his fingernails. His worth is not increased. His loved ones have simply lied to him to get him to perform. He has believed them, and he acts accordingly to purchase both his own self-respect and the love and approval of those around him.

A person who abuses his body by overeating in order to receive oral satisfaction, or some other love supply, is doing a wrong thing for a wrong reason. However, when he decides that his body is being abused, that it is ugly, that therefore he is not attractive to other people, and he decides to cease over-eating, goes on a diet, and is able to lose weight and put his body back into normal shape, he has done a right thing; he is no longer abusing his body, but he has done it for a wrong reason— that he might be attractive to other people and thereby have their approval and their love. That kind of love, based upon the acceptable shape of his body, is conditional and fake. It is a cheap substitute. He is doing a right thing for a wrong reason. His basic feelings of being insecure and inadequate and unloved probably have not changed at all.

The man who does not pay tithing because he "can't afford it" is doing a wrong thing for a wrong reason. When, however, he begins one day to pay tithing because his boss or his next-door neighbor has become his ward bishop, he is now doing a right thing, but for a wrong reason. His motivation is a deficiency one, and the love supply (the security and approval he gets from paying tithing) is not a real love supply but a purchased cheap substitute.

A third type of interaction is *doing right things for right reasons.* * This is action motivated by *being*. It is based in the respect for and the expression of the inside self, the heavenly being that inhabits the mortal body. Whatever action occurs expresses, nourishes, and strengthens that being, reinforcing its flowing power, acknowledging its presence and importance and contribution in all our thoughts and motivations. In this kind of interaction a person pays his tithes and offerings as an expression of his deepest love for his heavenly spirit. He would not abuse it, nor display it, nor prostitute it, nor destroy it. He knows that these things would violate his sacred identity. He relates to other people and their bodies on that same basis. He would give others real love supplies, motivated purely as expressions of his own precious being, never for gain nor for conquest. His interactions with others, based upon his correct self-concept, would guide him to relate sensitively to the inner beings of others, and the only payoff desired or received would be the deep solid joy that inevitably comes from acting in harmony with his true divine identity.

Genuine love is a *being* relationship—a relating of one person to another in a way that matches the true identity of each person. Genuine love requires that *both* persons be sensitive enough to be able to recognize authentic treatment and receptive enough to be able to receive it (and, conversely, assertive enough to consistently reject counterfeits).

Achieving genuine love demands more than simply *wanting* to help someone else change his self-concept—wanting to help him grow in moral insight, to become unselfish, to stop

---

* One often hears of a category called doing wrong things for right reasons. Actually, there is no such category. Allowing for the correctness of divine judgment, and even human judgment, a thing done for a right reason is a right thing. For instance, when Nephi killed Laban (1 Nephi 4:10-18), it was the right thing to do.

lying or overeating, or to cease being psychoneurotic, psycho-somatic, or sociopathic. Genuine love takes more than simple desire. One must be willing and able to give and receive true love supplies. One must *have them* to give. If his own love buckets are empty, he'll certainly not be able to fill someone else's. He cannot give what he does not have and does not know how to receive.

Fortunately, the giving and the receiving of true love supplies are skills that we have a lifetime to learn. And we *can* learn them, but it takes great desire and will. Always, the new power of repentance must equal the old power of falsehood. We have to match the power by which our substitute style orig-inated. A great railroad spike, driven into a timber with a huge sledgehammer, cannot be pulled out with a little carpenter's hammer. Our substitute styles, our false love definitions, our fake love supplies have been driven into us under great stress, by love deprivation, by emotional manipulation, by physical abuse, by ignorance, hate, lust, selfishness, deceit, anger, frustration. These powerful counterfeits are the great negative sledgehammers that have driven these spikes. Their negative power must be matched with an equal positive power.

We must begin with ourselves. We must desire first and foremost to understand what our own styles are and how they repay our allegiance. There is a simple formula for discerning payoffs that also demonstrates the fact that we do choose our styles. It is this. The negative self rationalizes:

1. I have to criticize others.
2. If I don't criticize others, I won't feel superior.
3. I'd rather criticize others than *not* feel superior.
4. Therefore, *I choose* to criticize.

The target here is to attain a pleasurable illusion of worth. The style is criticizing, and the payoff is a feeling of false superiority, a false self-respect, which is a fake love supply. The style fills the felt need. The style is deliberately chosen to achieve the acceptable payoff. The fact that one has actually chosen the style himself is crucial, for he might just as well choose another style, and may well do so, especially as life's tidal forces ebb and flow with each new independent situation.

This freedom to choose is a basic principle of our mortality. We are free to choose slavery or liberty. We are free to choose to be dependent, to be victimized, to be driven by false, substitute needs and styles, or to choose to be independent, free agents, functioning in being-motivated interactions. We choose our dynamics. We choose our styles. We even choose our wounds. We always choose what we judge to be the greater joy over the lesser pain. This is a law of our existence. But the greatest joy, the greatest positive "pay-off" in this world or out of it is the joy of being real, of being true to the heavenly reality within us, in other words, the joy of maintaining our spiritual first estate as we progress in the power of our mortal second estate.

Yet, even so, when we begin to understand that in this life we have not known some kinds of love supplies, and that, in their places, we have accepted various contrived substitutes, we are usually shocked and dismayed. Our negative self may tell us we are tied to our substitute styles and that we cannot change. But this is an untruth, for the same power that allows us to accept and be governed by our negative self also allows us to accept and to be governed by our real self.

The major irony about our acceptance of our love substitutes is that they actually steal away from us even more love than we intend them to produce. All of Satan's lies and deceptions multiply upon themselves. One may think that he is getting more love, but actually, he is not. He is getting less. A child who sucks his thumb in order to feel better is increasingly rejected as he continues his pattern. A person who is shy in order to protect himself from being rejected puts himself in a position of not being available to others to love. Substitute styles are simply defense systems that work by creating illusions that we choose to accept as real. They are part of Satan's plan to enslave and destroy us. They must be recognized, understood, and then changed so that we may achieve real happiness.

And is this not what we are here for—to learn to make real happiness ours, truly, and eternally? Is this not why the earth was created and men and women put upon it? And why the whole plan of salvation was instituted? The prophet Nephi said it briefly and beautifully when he said, "But behold, all things have been done in the wisdom of him who knoweth all things. Adam fell that men might be; and men are, that they might have joy." (2 Nephi 2:24-25.)

10

Discerning Our Ways

Enter ye in at the strait gate: for wide is the gate, and broad is the way, that leadeth to destruction, and many there be which go in thereat: Because strait is the gate, and narrow is the way, which leadeth unto life, and few there be that find it. (Matthew 7:13-14.)

When Jesus said that the second greatest commandment in the law was "Thou shalt love thy neighbour as thyself," he was stating a basic fact in the keeping of our first estate. We do indeed love others as we love ourselves. Love is action that accords with the reality of our own true identity and the true identities of other people as children of God. Love is reality treatment: genuine love can never be other than this. Achieving and learning to live by this love, wherein our souls are nourished by treatment that matches our spiritual identities, are two of our greatest opportunities.

Unfortunately, most of us seldom achieve this. Our life in the world—socially, economically, competitively—often creates in us wrong attitudes and wrong action patterns. In many areas of our lives we mutate until our hopes and wants are often no longer in accord with spiritual reality. We accept and

92

adopt styles that achieve substitute nourishment for substitute selves. Sometimes we even lose our spiritual perspective completely, and our original first estate changes to a world estate, where our motivations have become based upon earthly deficiency instead of heavenly being. When this happens, we have drifted from the narrow way of freedom and eternal happiness into the broad and crowded way which leads to destruction. Substitute styles destroy; they are manipulative of others and mutating to ourselves. They are tools of Satan and should be recognized as such. But they can be difficult to perceive.

There is such a fine line between deficiency and sufficiency motivations, between helping another person in order to get something from him or helping him as an expression of one's own inside self. A person who gives to get is usually a worried, desperate, concerned person. Like the mother who hugs her son in order to fill her own need, this person is driven by outside forces, by external measures of his purpose and worth. He is seldom in charge of his own experience. Most often he feels deficient and inadequate. Even when he does right things, he frequently does them for wrong reasons.

On the other hand, a person who gives to express his own being most often is doing right things for right reasons. He gives in order to express his own fullness; he strives to share from that fullness. He doesn't care whether he gets anything back or not. He is not worried or desperate. He celebrates every man's life as his own beauty. He loves others as he loves himself—and the more he appreciates his own great value and purpose, his own true beauty and availability, the more he appreciates other people's beauty, value, and availability.

The Lord proclaims, "For behold, this is my work and my glory—to bring to pass the immortality and eternal life of man." (Moses 1:39.) The positive person's work and glory are like the Lord's in that whatever help or service he extends is done as an expression of himself, of his own worth, never as a condition of it. He feels his worth, and what he does expresses that worth. His love for others, therefore, is not conditional. It is not based upon any external condition of another's worth or value to him. His love is based upon internal values, not external measurements. It is spiritual, for it surpasses the things of this world, the things of time and space, of appearances and performances. It is therefore eternal.

In everything we do we express our mixture of our "selves," our real self, and our negative substitute, world self. We are open books ready for the reading, but most of us do not try to read. Most of us blunder blindly along, insensitive and unaware of what is happening with us. Such insensitivity is not celestial. It is not maintaining our first estate. Strait *is* the gate and narrow *is* the way that leads to eternal life, and few there be that find it. Yet, there are many signs available to us along the way, signs that reveal the mixture we have accepted and the conflicts we endure.

For instance, such a common act as blushing at the least little thing may be a quiet sign of tension. It can indicate a self-conscious stress. We blush when we are frustrated or when we are enduring some form of emotional strain. If we blush often, we might ask ourselves, "What is the stress, and what is causing it?" Then we might make a list of all the things that make us blush. If we examine the list carefully, we will find some things occurring again and again. A pattern will emerge that will give us clues as to what things are threatening to us, what things create what kinds of tensions in us. Blushing itself is not the tension, although it can become a tension; actually, it is simply one more crutch that we have adopted to ease some problem, to release some tension, to escape some kind of pressure. If we wish to be free from this crutch, we must find out why we prefer it over actually solving the problem. Why do we tolerate the tension? A crutch always aids a toleration. Blushing is a substitute style, allowing us to evade and tolerate instead of control and handle. Blushing satisfies to some extent some need of a substitute identity, a substitute self, that is being accepted by us in place of our real self.

In almost any situation, it is easy for our negative, world

selves to take control, protected and encouraged as they are by the clutter and refuse of our worldly lives. But if we are sensitive and aware, we can discern signs and symptoms so that we can be in control. These symptoms inevitably relate to external, quantitative, worldly things rooted in feelings of deficiency, inadequacy, and uncertainty.

For instance, there are people who are so inadequate in themselves that they are terrified to be alone. They are constantly doing, and going, and associating. It's almost as if they felt that inside their jungle was some beast, threatening, lurking, from which they had to constantly escape. They are always playing games, or going to a movie, or to a play, or on a tour, or on a vacation, or to visit someone, or to see something. They endeavor to live vicariously. They seek company to avoid themselves. Yet, in reality, when such people honestly begin to examine what they are doing and why they are doing it, they find that they are as afraid of other people as they are of themselves. They feel threatened on all sides. They can't stand being alone and they can't stand being together. They discover that their negative self-concept makes them feel negative even toward those in whom they seek protection.

Indecision is another symptom of conflict between our selves. For instance, many young people cannot decide to pursue further education; or, having already been pushed to technical school or to the university, they cannot choose a major; or, after graduation, they cannot choose a job. They feel doubtful—they feel that someday, after they get into school, or into a major, or into a job, their choices will prove to be unsuitable. They are very unsure. They have lost faith in themselves. They do not trust their own inner voice to make right decisions. Some people are so unsure of themselves that they are afraid even to answer the telephone. They fear that they will say the wrong thing, or that they will stutter, or stammer, or not know what to say. They have lost their original confidence and faith in their original identity, in their own powerful spiritual being. They cannot make decisions because inside of them there has grown a great substitute negative voice that says over and over again, "It won't work out. It's not right for you. You can't succeed."

A companion symptom to indecision is moodiness. People who have accepted their substitute negative selves as their real selves are often very moody. They are caught in a world of exaggeration. They exaggerate the negative in their lives in order to get sympathy (which in such cases is a love substitute). They find a counterfeit reassurance in recounting their unhappy experiences. They dwell upon negative things. They are like those people who make a crutch out of therapy, who enjoy sorting out their garbage piles and love to wallow in their own mess. Often, such moody people have deep wounds. They are often very fragile and easily broken. They are touchy. They have never really found out what is going on inside of them, or how to reduce their stresses and pressures by honesty, by knowledge, by faith and prayer, and by understanding. They have never found out how to relieve the pressure underneath their layers, how to find their real self beneath all their clutter and refuse and defenses, and how to free that self, and nourish it, and allow it to enrich their lives.

A person who has become enslaved to the styles of his substitute self must become aware of what he is doing. He must catch himself each time the negative in him swings into action. He must not continue to let these things happen, for each time he allows the negative style to occur, it pays off by reinforcing his negative substitute self, strengthening the muffling layers that cover his real self. With determination and vigor, he must say to himself, aloud if necessary, "Just a minute now; I just told a lie." Then he must say to himself, "Why did I tell that lie? What did I expect to get from that?" And then he must say, "Is it really worth it to me to have that?"

The recognition of what he's doing, even the saying of it aloud, is the process of discovering and freeing the real self, for it is the real self that speaks when those assertive questions are asked. And it is the positive self that will answer these questions honestly and correctly. The positive self lives the heavenly laws. It can only function by the requirements of its first estate. By catching the negative style and exposing it, one strengthens his positive self. In time, he can actually force the negative identifications to stop, and he will be able to comfortably give these tasks over to his real self.

The questions and the procedure for the analysis are always the same. For instance, for some people, money is equated with worth. They have marital problems because they are short of money. They have emotional problems because of bankruptcy. They even end their lives, convinced of their own purposelessness and lack of value because of lack of money. They measure their needs in money, or the lack of it, and consequently, their wants are out of proportion.

I have a little boy who is just eight years old, and when he goes downtown all he has in his pockets is his small allowance, yet he wants everything he sees. He says to me, "I want this truck. I want this ball. I want this bat. I want this catcher's mitt." And he comes up with very complex ways to get them.

"Well," he says, "I can borrow so much from Julie. And I can borrow so much from Amy. And then I can get some more from Paul. I will do this for money, and I will do that. And if you loan me a dollar and twenty-eight cents, I promise I will clean the garage." He is like many people who seek to buy a new car or a new house that they cannot afford.

I say to him, "David, wouldn't it be much simpler to just fix your wanter?"

He is puzzled, and he replies, "But Daddy, how do I do that? I don't know how to do that. How do I fix my wanter?"

And my explanation to him is the same as my explanation to older people who are yet having the same kind of problems. I tell him, in simple terms, that the first thing he must do is find out what these things mean to him. Why must he have them? What do they bring to him? What is their payoff?

One adult person says to me, "Well, that shiny new car means that I am somebody." Another person says, "That big house I'm living in means that I have made it in life. When friends come to see me, my house shows them what a success I am." The "want" is not the object itself, but what the object pays off. And when the want is giant and overexaggerated and material, when getting and possessing means safety and security and worth, then one can be sure that he is involved in employing a crutch, a substitute style, for some purpose and in some way. For the man with the new car, for the man with the big house, even for little David, it is a money crutch.

There are as many different crutches as there are negative selves to support. Some people have reading crutches, scholarly crutches, employment crutches, profession crutches. All of these otherwise valid activities or interests become crutches when they pay off in a false feeling of worth.

In a money crutch, one's worth is tied up in his money. The man who purchased the big new car did not buy the car simply to transport him to some destination. Transportation was, of course, one of his payoffs, but not his primary one. He really bought the car to show himself off. Many people follow this same pattern with their clothing. They don't use clothing to cover their precious and sacred body, but instead use clothing to show off that body, to obtain a payoff of attention, or allegiance, or power. The same pattern appears in overeating, where food is not used to nourish the body, but instead is used as a crutch to buy sympathy, or attention, or to satisfy some other unmet need.

What does a person do when he becomes aware of his crutches? There are several things. Depending upon the desired payoff, he might change them, exchanging one, perhaps, for another more available, or perhaps more socially acceptable, or more moral. Or he might journey deep into his value systems and his past experience and determine the source of his use and acceptance of the crutch. He might ask himself, "What does money do for me? What are the jobs of my spirit self that I am using money to accomplish?" Then he must try to give these jobs back to his spirit self.

A man said to me the other day, "When I get uptight and nervous, I drink soda pop. I smoke cigarettes. I drink coffee. I chew gum. I suck the end of my pencil. When I get frightened,

I bite my fingernails." What is he really saying? He is saying that when he gets under stress and tension, he gives the jobs of handling his anxiety to his mouth. His style is called oral gratification. When he is under pressure, instead of talking these pressures over with someone, finding out what is going wrong, what he is frightened of, what sort of inadequacies he feels he has—instead of taking strength in his real identity and acting accordingly in confidence—he turns to a substitute style. He sucks, he eats, he bites, he chews, he gives the jobs of his spirit self over to his mouth. It is a poor substitute; his body and his mind suffer thereby.

It is the same with those who use money, or clothing, or food, or any number of things, as crutches. False feelings of purpose and worth are accepted in the place of those genuine feelings that the spiritual identity of each of us is meant to satisfy. The resultant emotional bankruptcy and spiritual emptiness are inevitable, for true happiness is a fullness that comes in living the laws of God, the laws of our reality, the laws of our first estate. True happiness cannot be bought with money, nor with food, nor with pacifiers such as cigarettes or coffee, nor with college degrees, nor uniforms, nor awards, nor any such earthly and outward things.

The greatest achievement in the world is to become honest with one's self and thereby with others, to live by truth and reality. A healthy person seeks to do this. He knows that real love is based on reality and truth, not protection or safety. And he senses his own great need for this genuine love to nourish his spirit and give him true happiness.

But few of us wholly achieve this high ideal—we are not so completely healthy. We often deceive ourselves, and even take solace in our deceptions. Small things grow out of all proportion. For example, some of us are very time conscious. We become quite disturbed when other people are late to a function, or perhaps disturb proceedings by their tardiness. We become upset at ourselves when we don't accomplish certain jobs within a certain time. For us, the importance of the earth's dimension of time has become exaggerated. It has become disproportionate. Perhaps, when we were small, someone drilled into us with great emotional power that our being punctual was a condition of our worth. We were made to believe that only scoundrels are late, that people who are not on time are inconsiderate, selfish, rude, and mean. In short, we have come to believe that later-comers have less worth than on-timers. Actually, that kind of thinking is not honest; it may be a lie. Being late isn't bad. It *is* inconsiderate, but it is not immoral. And it does not decrease in the slightest anyone's value as a person.

Interestingly enough, there are those who make being constantly late as much of a crutch for themselves as being on time is for some others. These people intend to come late. They say to themselves, "I love to have everyone look at me. When I disrupt the proceedings, people notice me. This gives me a feeling of importance. I need that feeling. Therefore, I will plan it that way."

In both situations, being on time and being late, the payoff is attaining a feeling of superiority, or control, or self-righteousness, all of which are conditions of personal worth. The style is either being on time or being late. But in either case, the self-concept is negative, for the style implies a need for external things to bolster one's feelings of worth.

I had a patient once who told me that her mother used to swat her on the legs with a clothes hanger, one swat for every minute past thirty minutes that she didn't have the dishes done. Later on, when she was older, if she came home one minute late from a date, she was grounded for a week. Such punishment as this was inordinate; it was exaggerated; it was out of proportion. Her mother really should have overlooked much of this kind of behavior. But regardless, this was the model the young girl had to follow, and because her mother had made such a big thing out of being on time, the girl now found that she was torn: she hated time and needed to rebel against it, yet it had become a condition of her own worth and she could not live with her own rebellion. Being on time had become a crutch upon which she leaned to feel her own worth and goodness.

Many people do this same sort of thing with cleanliness, with neatness, with orderliness. Some women cannot sleep at night if the dishes are not completely done and the kitchen swept and clean. Others cannot rest until the ironing is done, or the washing is done, or until the house is immaculately clean. Only when they have accomplished these things can they go to bed and sleep, feeling good inside of themselves. These performances, while good and excellent in their proper places, have for them become crutches upon which they base their feelings of worth, not only as wives and mothers, but also as persons.

Any performance reflects our inner thinking and judgment. Those things that bother us about our own performance also bother us about other people's performance. Our irritation at others' crutches is a key for detecting our own crutches. The things that bother us in other people are more than often in ourselves. We often share the same biases. For instance, if you dislike people who are late, you yourself probably have a great fear of being late, or, perhaps, you yourself may actually be late quite often. If you disdain people who are not good house-keepers, or whose dishes sit in the sink, or who do not clean up their kitchens or fold their washing or iron their clothing, you will probably find that inside yourself you have a great fear of not being adequate yourself in these areas: and perhaps, actually, you may *not* be adequate in these areas.

In diagnosing problems of people who are antagonistic toward other people, psychologists often use a sentence completion test. One of the sentences for completion says, "The things I hate most in other people are. . ." Often people will write in the blanks after this question a complete diagnosis of their own antagonisms, for the things they hate in others, they hate in themselves. Hate is a most terrible thing, a powerful, disruptive, emotional experience. It is the reverse of love. People who hate others hate themselves. A life filled with hate is a miserable, lonely, empty life. People who adopt hate as a style build their own jail; they live in their own private prison, and they suffer their own private horror in a self-made outer darkness.

The converse of the rule is equally true, for the things we love most in others are the things we love in ourselves. The Lord's statement about loving others as we love ourselves is a statement of fact even more than it is a commandment.

Because we are so much *of* the world, our substitute selves tend to take over. Our interrelationships are often ruled more by degrees of hate than they are by degrees of love. Hostility, inadequacy, possessiveness, misused protectiveness, misused sexuality, jealousy, revenge—all these styles too often rule our relationships.

We learn these manipulative styles when we are very young. For instance, a child often learns to use hostility to get a counterfeit form of love. He needs genuine love, but he becomes willing to accept counterfeits. He finds that he can get attention if he is antagonistic, shouting back at his mother that she doesn't really love him. Now, if the mother is secure in herself and knows that she truly does love her child, his remark will have no effect upon her. But if she is not sure about her own feelings, if really she is worried as to whether she loves her child as she ought, or whether she is an adequate mother or not, her child's accusation can be extremely disturbing to her. The child has found her wound, and, because she hurts, he will get the attention that he desires. In time hostility, and perhaps even hate, will become an acceptable style that he may employ to achieve this counterfeit for real love.

Hostility, as a style, can take many forms in our lives. It may appear as antagonism, criticizing, faultfinding, or nit-picking; it may take the forms of silent treatment, withdrawal, frigidity; or it may appear as active, physically destructive revenge. People who choose hostility as a style have wounds that they protect by hurting others. They have taught themselves to feel safe in another's pain, to feel superior in another's misery. The actively hostile person deliberately wounds another for his own benefit. His joy and security are in seeing another person rejected and hurt. Yet, he really hurts himself more than he hurts others. Underneath his hostility is anger, and underneath his anger is pain. He seeks to revenge himself, and he feels that his hurt is vindicated if he can hurt others.

Hostility, as a style, should be examined by its user to find out what its real purposes are and why he chooses to use it. It is a terribly powerful style. Most people use it more than they are willing to recognize. Properly used, hostility (in the form of firmness or assertiveness, for instance) can protect a nation, a society, a home, a family, or an individual from invasion or devastation. Improperly used, it can destroy all of these and even the group or individual who chooses to employ it.

In the home, hostility frequently becomes a manipulative force. It is most often conditional. Parents use it to threaten their children to get them to perform according to demand. And children, following their parental models, turn the same weapon upon their parents and their brothers and sisters. Julie's mother, who was so offended by Julie's forgetful delay in setting the Sunday table, used hostility to make Julie feel bad and, hopefully, to get her to hurry and to change her ways. In time, though, Julie may use the same hostile style to get her mother to perform for her. She may scream at her mother, call her names, and even slap her, if it will pay off in making Julie feel superior, more free, or more able. Hostility breeds hostility, even as hate breeds hate. Those who use hostility almost always receive hostility in return.

Some parents unwittingly become hostile toward their children when the children bring their friends into the home. Often this is because the parents' privacy is threatened or their material goods are endangered by the children's awkwardness, carelessness, or lack of restraint. Some parents use hostility to defend their own self-image as "good parents"; they direct hostility toward well-meaning teachers and neighbors or anyone who dares to correct or criticize their misbehaving children.

Feelings of hostility are easily transferred from one situation to another, or from one person to another. Children often do this when they begin attending school. Although the child may never have seen his new teacher before, he is able to transfer many of the feelings he has toward his mother to his teacher. This happens easily because the teacher is big and she is usually female and she is in charge. Antagonism is more quickly apparent than affection, and though she may be a perfect teacher, kind and loving and competent, she will still have to live through this hostility transference experience. The child will not stop treating her as he treats his mother until he finds out that she is not like his mother. It will be up to the teacher to show the child the differences. She will need to carefully find out why he is doing whatever he is doing. She must be careful not to take his actions personally and return his hostility, for this will confirm to him the correctness of his transference. She must be sensitive enough to know that he is blindly bringing hostility from his home toward her. She must be wise enough to know that she, as an individual person, is not really in the situation at all. When the child recognizes her identity, disassociated from his former experience, he will cease his hostility toward her.

Parents sometimes transfer hostility from one child to another. Often they project the unsatisfactory performances of older children onto younger children. A young woman in one of my classes told me that her mother constantly quarreled with her. Any kind of public performance by the daughter was a signal for hostility from her mother. The daughter could not go on a date, take part in a play, or go out with her crowd without going through scenes of threatening, shouting, and sometimes days of sulking and silence. Everything that the girl did was suspect. In talking with her, I found out that she had two older brothers who had openly violated the mother's deepest religious beliefs, and had done so publicly. Because the mother used the older brothers' behavior to measure her success as a mother (and also as a person), she felt diminished in her own personal worth. It was easy to defend her hurt with hostility, and very easy to transfer her style of hostility toward her sons to her relationship with her daughter, who, in reality, was faithful in every respect to the religious beliefs the mother prized so highly. Instead of loving the daughter for her own individual value and receiving love in return, the mother, in her fear and

transferred hostility, was forcing the daughter into a consideration of the very patterns and styles she hated so much in the
lives of her sons.

I once sent a girl with whom I had had a comfortable
counseling relationship to experience some group therapy. In
about ten minutes she came back as white and pale as she could
be. I said to her, "Eileen, you are supposed to be in that group.
What's wrong?"

She replied, "I'll never go to that group again."

"Why not?" I asked. "There should be no problems for you.
There are both male and female therapists working together
with that group."

She began to cry. "That's the trouble," she said. "It's just
like my family. The group is run by a mother and a father and
there are three boys and four girls up there. I couldn't stay. I felt
so terrible inside. I couldn't stand it."

And so she had run away because she felt so threatened, so
afraid. She had transferred her hostility toward her family to
the group even though there really wasn't any hostility there at
all.

Transferences are destructive because they are out of touch
with reality. When one transfers feelings from one person to
another person, he does not give the second person a chance to
be his own self. He refuses to see the second person's real
identity. In a sense, he makes him into somebody else, and
therefore actions toward him cannot match true facts.

Heaven is a social place. One of our greatest assignments in
keeping our spiritual first estate through our earthly second
estate is in learning how to truly love our brothers and sisters no
matter what their role in our mortal lives—father, mother,
teacher, friend, son, or daughter. We must be able to see other
people as they really are and treat them accordingly. We must
not make them into something they are not. We must therefore
learn how to analyze the styles of behavior we have adopted,
recognizing why we do what we do, knowing precisely what
rewards we expect, what kind of nourishment comes, and what
aspects of ourselves are being fed thereby. We must enter the

strait gate of eternal reality that leads to life, and turn away from the broad, deceptive way of the world that leads only to misery and destruction.

11

Male and Female

And God said, Let us make man in our image, after our likeness: and let them have dominion . . . over all the earth. . . . So God created man in his own image, in the image of God created he him; male and female created he them. And God blessed them, and God said unto them, Be fruitful, and multiply, and replenish the earth, and subdue it. (Genesis 1:26-28.)

When God created man, he created him in the image of the great future that man is capable of attaining. He created man male and female, each self-adequate and self-sufficient to mutually contribute to a wholeness of being that is the very image of God. Man's mortality continues this creation by offering to men and women varied and appropriate experiences that teach them and shape them, providing growing room so that they may become in very deed and fact like their heavenly parents.

Satan is determined to destroy that magnificent potential inherent in each one of us by undermining our individual confidence in ourselves as valuable, beautiful, and infinitely able men and women. One of his most successful ways of doing this is to convince us that we are not sufficient, not adequate, that we do not measure up to some world measure for "real" maleness or "real" femaleness, that we need some crutch to bolster us, some counterfeit supply to nourish us—that we need to do this act, or say this thing, or wear this costume, or anoint our bodies with this ointment, or paint our faces with this or that color in this or that fashion—in short, that we need to lie to ourselves and to others so that none will know how deeply inadequate we think we are. He would change us into strange misshapen creatures, far different from the capable whole persons we were originally created to be—bright beings of light, male and female, inherently adequate and sufficient, freely capable of becoming mutually contributive to a wholeness that is Godlike, indeed, that is the very image of God. And Satan has been successful, for in our time, male and female feelings of inadequacy have become so prevalent and powerful that, coupled with false societal pressures and attitudes, they threaten our very civilization, striking at the roots of marriage and family. Today they are major sources for our human misery and are tremendously destructive.

Before a person can find out what it means to be a male or a female, he must find out what it means to be a person. The spirit self, the heavenly being that dwells inside every male or female body, is in harmony with that body. Maleness and femaleness extend beyond the outward form of the flesh. Indeed, the body is in the form of the spirit that inhabits it; it is not the other way around. The second estate depends upon the first estate. The spirit precedes the body and rules over it, or should do. Our body is in the form of our spirit. Heavenly Father's house is a house of order.

Because all spirits, both male and female, are persons, all can do most things that human persons do. Women can build houses. Men can love babies. Women can earn money. Men can bake bread. These things, each can do by right of his personhood. But there are specialties, things that are specific and precious, that belong appropriately to only one sex. For instance, a human female has specialties. She can do some things better than any male because she is a female.

One great female specialty is tenderness. Women find it easier to be concerned with feelings than with tasks. They find it easier to be gentle, soft, forgiving, understanding. A healthy female finds it easy to love a new little baby because she has a deep spiritual sensitivity to the real identity of the baby's being. It is natural to treat things of great value with great tenderness and great care. In the healthy woman who knows herself, this sensitivity to great value is very strong. She therefore loves being with the baby and doing for it. When a baby cries, she senses what kind of a cry it is, and she feels what she should do to help. She has a special joy in doing it. It is not a burden. She is not driven to do it. Girls who rebel against such activities and interests as these usually have been forced or abused in them. Girls who have been freely allowed to be real persons and therefore real females find that these sensitivities and capabilities flow in them without compulsion.

Healthy females never compare nor belittle their female specialties in the light of some male specialty. They have no interest in being male. Nor does a healthy male person have any interest in being female. Healthy people are happy to be who they are. They love their identities so much that they would never trade. Those who are truly unhappy in their identities are those who have been abused in some way—by false identities, by substitute styles, by counterfeit demands forced upon them by mutated persons who basically dislike themselves. Insensitive parents perhaps have said, "You are a girl, so you must do the dishes," or "You are a boy, so you must empty the garbage." Insensitive husbands may have said, "You are a woman, so you must wash the dirty diapers. You must clean the house. You must fix the meals." And insensitive wives have said to husbands, "You are a man, so you must handle the money. You must make all the decisions. You must tell me what to do. You must be big and strong. You must earn more money; you must buy me a bigger house, or a finer car, or more clothing."

But this is not the way it should be. Maleness or femaleness should flow from the thrill of knowing and rejoicing in one's inner identity. It should flow from the inside outward, from internal to external. Any other way is a misuse, counterfeit, and eternally destructive to the soul.

Males also have specialties. Logically enough, their major specialty is power. A male has a strong body with climactic strength, which works well over a short period of time. He can build houses. He can carry heavy loads. He can plow. He can dig. He loves responsibility. He loves good management. He admires capable administration. He is good at making decisions. He likes to make things work for him. He likes to protect and provide. These are male specialties. He doesn't *have* to do them. He isn't driven by them, or at least he ought not to be. They are strengths and attributes that flow from his maleness.

When a man is prohibited from making good decisions, from expressing his power properly, from being good at external tasks, from fixing things, from protecting his women and his children from attack, from danger, from hunger and cold; when he is prohibited from doing these things by being criticized, being downgraded, and, perhaps, at last even being replaced by a mother or wife who takes over and makes all the decisions, his identity as a male person is being threatened.

Likewise, when a wife is prevented from being the woman she was intended to be—when she is not allowed to express her womanhood in gentleness and compassion, in understanding and feeling, in having a family and taking care of it, in loving and helping, in training and teaching her children, in serving and growing, in contributing toward decisions, in helping set goals and reaching them *with* her husband—her identity is inhibited. She is kept from being the woman she was meant to be, and her inner female being is stifled.

In either case, male or female, the person who was meant to be is being smothered and perverted, and he soon begins to feel inadequate and incapable. Before long, he is very unhappy.

Unhappy people who doubt their adequacy to be lovable and capable find it very easy to doubt their special individuality as male or female. Often they try to compensate by denying the physical, psychological, and spiritual differences in the sexes.

The modern concept of unisex that promotes the point of view that there are no differences between male and female, that male and female specialties are not inherent, but learned, is but one more of Satan's many counterfeits, created to blind men and women to the truth about themselves. Unisex justifies and rationalizes; it prevents men and women from perceiving that such sexual interactions are not authentic, but are merely compensations for feelings of deficiency and frustration.

When a person compensates by switching sexual roles, it is called mixing sexualities. Behavior ranges from adopting the other sex's clothing, styles, or way of life, to extraordinary or violent deviance. Homosexuality, either male or female, is an extreme expression of mixed-up sexuality. Homosexuals have become convinced that sexual contact is simply a way to express affection; it is a safe way to prove that one is lovable and capable. Homosexuals have lost the primal vision that sex is a sacred procreative power that is meant to create an emotional unity between male and female that is achieved in no other way—a permanent, self-perpetuating, eternal family relationship in the very image of God.

Unisexuality in all its varied forms and guises, from sexual competition to sodomy and lesbianism, is meant to compensate for feelings of inadequacy or deficiency. It is fraught with eternally destructive consequences. Contrary to the gospel of Jesus Christ, it denies the infinite significance of maleness and femaleness and the eternal permanence of the family, thereby thwarting the spirit in its progress toward Godhood.

Inadequacy, deficiency, and frustration, in either male or female, are efficient tools in the hands of Satan because they verify the negative self. They leave great hunger holes that throb for filling, even though the filling may be counterfeit. They demand that a style be found that will compensate, that will satisfy. Almost anything may prove acceptable, but more often than not, the style that is chosen has to do with sexual relationships.

A crying wife comes in for counsel; she reports that her husband says she is frigid. In the next appointment, her husband comes in and says that he must be oversexed. Both wife and husband are confused and dismayed. They have had a happy marriage, but now they seem headed toward separation and divorce. Each blames the other, and each takes refuge in feeling that he cannot help his inborn nature. But in actuality, this couple has begun to use sex and withdrawal from sex as styles to satisfy other needs.

Most often the pattern goes like this: The husband is facing emotional pressure or stress. He may be losing his job, or be threatened with bankruptcy. His maleness is being threatened. Because his wife is available, and morally and socially acceptable, he begins to use her to fill his private, unmet, emotional need. Sex satisfies his need for power and control. But his wife, as a person, resents being so used. In order to handle her negative feelings, she withdraws. At this point, the husband may decide that his life has become so busy that he and his wife are drifting apart. As he begins to realize the growing gap in their communication, his maleness is threatened on a second level, and he begins to use sex to give him an illusion of closeness and security in his marriage. But his use of sex in these substitute ways is futile. It is, in fact, destructive, and only drives him and his wife further apart. His wife may have had a reasonably healthy outlook about sex and marital relations before, but now the present situation causes resentment in her, and she handles this by adopting a style of passive rebellion, by withdrawing, or by refusing to cooperate.

When men or women are using sex as a style to satisfy other needs, several key things usually happen. There is inconsiderateness. There is an increase in demand and frequency. There is an inordinate interest in sexual things and practices. Sexuality becomes very important, and sexual relations become a primary necessity. These are signs that sex is being misused. Healthy people do not depend so heavily on sex. To a healthy person, sex is a minor part of his relationship with his wife; sexual relations are not an everyday necessity. But in a sick relationship, an inordinate amount of sex becomes a throbbing necessity, and when it does not occur, there is fussing and fuming and fighting and trouble in the marriage. Such demand and such controversy are sure signs of a crutch. They indicate, without a doubt, that someone in the relationship is becoming dependent upon sex as a crutch to help him or her over some stress or feeling of inadequacy. In the case of the couple who came to see me, it was the frustrated husband. Ralph would say in a tight, brittle tone, "Now look here, Mary, this is the sixth day. We are *not* going to go on like this." Mary would begin to cry, and before the hour was over, she would have successfully rejected him by passive aggression, refusing to cooperate. As the tension mounted higher, and the estrangement spread wider, the separation became more and more difficult to halt.

Mary's resentment at Ralph's treatment of her is normal and predictable. When women find themselves in such misuse relationships (both in marriage and outside of marriage), their sensitivity as females becomes very acute and defensive. They are quick to resent being used (unless they are using in return). Whether they understand it or not, they sense that their relationship with their partner is lopsided. The husband may say, "But, Mary, I love you so much that I want to have sex with you every day." Mary almost instinctively replies, "Well, I don't feel right about it. I don't think it's love to drive somebody, or push them, or force them. That isn't love to me." Though her husband may truly think that it *is* love that drives him, he is fooling himself. It is not love; it is need and use. Finally, it is performance as a sex partner that he requires, and that performance has nothing to do with the inner identity of his mate. He is merely using sex as a substitute style to compensate for his own deep feelings of inadequacy, or to make himself think he is getting close, or to get something somehow that fills his great hunger hole, his great deficiency need. Of course, his wife loses interest. Why should she be interested? She's not even in it. At most, she does what she may call her "wifely duties," and that's that.

Such a sexual relationship, whether male, female, or mutually imposed, soon shows every sign of use as a crutch:

inconsiderateness, increased frequency, inordinate interest, desperation, irritation, selfishness, arguments, bargains, and deals. It is destructive and leads only to misery.

Ralph and Mary are in trouble because they are out of tune with reality. Sex was never meant to carry the kind of load that they have put upon it. It was not meant to be used in that way. It was not meant to be abused. Sex in marriage is one way to express an emotional kinship within a permanent and responsible union. (It is in such a union that procreation ought always to occur; a baby deserves to be conceived in love, with a stable, permanent home and family to grow up in.) The sexual relationship, properly used, is spontaneous, positive, emotional, and fulfilling. It is akin to weeping with another person. A healthy person, male or female, in the midst of intense emotion, whether positive or negative, will cry, especially if the stress is a new kind of experience. But he never *schedules* crying. He doesn't plan it. He doesn't think about it. He isn't obsessed with it. He doesn't read books about it. He doesn't study to learn new techniques of crying. He doesn't talk about it all the time, nor joke about it. He doesn't go to see movies about it. He doesn't use crying to get things from other people, to manipulate, enslave, and destroy. And yet this beautiful, sweet expression of his deepest innermost feelings does come, and it fulfills and replenishes and strengthens as it was meant to do—as every expression of our real being does.

In our time and society, we abuse and misuse sex. We load it up with assignments it was not meant to fulfill. We expect it to answer all our needs, to meet all kinds of strange demands. In our time, maleness and femaleness are supposed to be proved by sexual contact. Sex is supposed somehow to establish virility. It is supposed to create power. It is supposed to create worth and purpose. One young wife said to me with great intensity, "Why, sex is my femaleness, my greatest purpose and meaning." And a young husband stated, "The sex act is *the* ultimate expression of love." An older woman sobbed, "Sex means to me that I am not getting old anymore. It proves that I still have something left." A husband laughed self-consciously, "Well, it gets me away from boredom."

Such loads as these are huge loads to put on such a little wagon. Sex cannot handle such things as maleness, femaleness, virility, power, intimacy, worth, purpose, even delivery from boredom—and when such big loads are put on such a tiny wagon, the wagon breaks down; it's as simple as that. When Ralph and Mary sit in my office, miserable and angry, and Ralph snarls, "She's frigid, that's all," and Mary snaps back, "He's oversexed, that's all," what's really happened is that they've broken their sex wagon by forcing it to carry a load that it simply could not hold. Sex was never intended to hold that kind of a giant psychological load.

Both Ralph and Mary are accepting a counterfeit reality. Their treatment of each other is far from loving; it is not congruent with what is really so. They have forgotten their true identities, and they are perverting the true identity and purpose of their marriage. They have made sex into an external substitute style and are now expecting it to produce an internal payoff. Their marriage is anything but celestial. Unless they change their directions and perspectives, their interactions will become more and more miserable. Soon they will avoid tensions by not going to bed at the same time. Ralph will stay up watching TV, reading, or doing something, and Mary will hurry to bed so she won't be awake when her husband comes upstairs. Or perhaps the roles will be reversed—Mary will stay up sewing, cleaning, or working at something, and Ralph will go to bed early, dead tired and perhaps angry. Soon Mary and Ralph will cease to pray together, and even to talk together. They are in a miserable cycle. And the day may come when Ralph or Mary may go elsewhere, attempting with someone else to get the sex wagon fixed. But such a new style outside of marriage can never fix the problem or ease the tension. It only makes it worse.

In actuality, Ralph and Mary need to sit down together, with counsel if such seems necessary, and examine their relationship. They need to understand what is happening to them. They need to get their perspectives and their behavior consonant with their identities. Selfishness, quarreling, inconsiderateness, abuse, all of these things are not the activities of the inside soul. These are not of God. They are of this world and have to do with the negative self and its substitute styles. When they understand this, their treatment of each other and of themselves will change.

A very intelligent and sensitive young woman was going with a young man who had developed a style in which sexual activity had become a substitute love supply. One day he said to her, "Well, Louise, we have been going together off and on for nearly six months. Isn't it about time for us to have a sexual relationship?"

"Now, just a minute," she replied. "I told you that I wasn't that kind of girl. I don't want that kind of relationship. I want to relate to you as a person, alive, real, and individual." And then she tried to explain to him what she understood a real courtship and marriage relationship to be; but he, like many young men throughout time, replied with such things as "If you really loved me, you would do it," and "I can't take you out anymore if you won't go to bed with me," and so on.

Finally, she said, "Now look, let's suppose that we do have a physical relationship. After you get through with my body, what will you do with the rest of me?"

He looked at her, surprised, and said, "You mean there's more?"

"Yes," she said wearily. "There's more. What are you going to do with that part of me that might want to be the mother of your children, and that part of me that should want to be with you all the year round for the rest of your life? And that part of me that is probably going to crash your car and overdraw your bank account? Don't you see that I am a person? I am somebody's sister. I am somebody's daughter. I eat, I hurt, and I cry. I am a person, don't you see? I am a girl person."

But he could not, or would not, understand. He had never thought about all these things. All he had thought about was his girl friend's body and how it might be used to meet his needs, or at least what he had come to believe were his needs. He didn't know her real identity and, in actuality, didn't *want* to know it.

Feelings of personal inadequacy are the most prevalent contributors to such misused sexual relationships. Both men and women suffer from these negative and false self attitudes that are always based in, and compensated by, an over-dependence on external things as measured by the world.

Styles used to fill these empty places depend upon the person and the situation. They appear variously and inter-changeably.

Three common substitute styles often used by women to compensate for feelings of female inadequacy are over-indulgence, seduction, and substitution (abandoning female-ness and substituting maleness in its place).

For instance, female inadequacy may begin with the woman's fear that she will not be "a good mother," that her children are not going to turn out "right." She may then begin to hate being at home with her children, and she may try to solve these feelings by substituting, by getting a job and leaving the family situation. Or she may indulge herself by overeating, becoming fat, escaping being a female and maybe also a mother. Or she may worry herself into bodily illness, compel-ling her children, by her overindulgence, to stay home, or perhaps compelling her husband to take the children out of the home.

She may begin to feel inadequate as a wife. She may feel that she is no longer beautiful, or no longer satisfactory to her husband. She may then begin to extend herself sexually. She may strive to become seductive. She may decide that her femininity has something to do with the way she performs in bed, or something to do with her size, her shape, or the style of clothes she wears.

Or she may withdraw. She may become shy. She may seek to protect herself by avoiding all interactions with everyone. She may even react antagonistically, attempting to forfeit her own specialties as a female and take over the specialties of her husband. She may compete with him in doing his male things. She may become bossy. She may become whiny, defensive, and full of complaints.

She may join two of these styles together and become a "supermother," using nurturance as a condition of her own worth, spoiling her children in order to get assurance that she is loved and is adequate. She will strive with all her might to make her children's lives her life, locking them to her and making them dependent upon her so that she is safe. As she moves deeper into this dual style, she may abandon her husband by competing with him, negating him, or making him into one of the children. She will be both overprotective and overindulgent. "My children mean everything to me," she will proclaim. "They are my motherhood. They are me." She will attempt to fill her own inadequacies by changing her identity and the identities of her loved ones.

Three common substitute styles used by men to compensate for feelings of male inadequacy are chauvinism (justifying all, including sexual abuse, by "male nature"), physicality (false toughness, bossiness), and vocational dominance (making job or profession primary over all else).

Male inadequacy may begin with a husband's fear that he is not adequate to provide for his family, that he is not able to compete on the world's labor market, or that he is not capable of loving or fathering his family, and is therefore somehow less than male. He may begin to feel that he is a burden to his wife and to his children, or that they are a burden to him. He may bolster his "maleness" by withdrawing from them, and by seeking companionship with other women who do not threaten him, emotionally or financially. Or he may retreat into his profession or his vocation. In extreme situations, he may desert his family altogether.

He may become forceful at home, irritable, cross, bossy. He may become harsh with the children or critical and negative toward his wife. He may become inconsiderate and demanding in his sexual relationships with her. He may wheedle, bribe, and bargain to get her to try to satisfy his misplaced sexual demands. He may even become physically violent or abusive. He may turn his hostility toward others, becoming fiercely competitive in his vocation or harsh and abusive with his co-workers. He may proclaim his maleness with other crutches, such as liquor or drugs. He may become competitive with his wife and her motherhood, becoming a "superfather," making motherliness and nurturance a condition of his worth.

Or he may even prove himself impotent in sex relations with his wife, perhaps to put her down or to prove to her that he is in charge. Impotence can happen in situations where the wife too is feeling inadequate and is using sex to prove to herself that her marriage is still good and that her husband still loves her. When she demands a certain level of sexual performance from her husband to prove her female adequacy and the adequacy of their union, the husband often reacts with passive hostility. He becomes impotent, leaving his wife unhappy and unfulfilled, and falsely proving by passive aggression his mistaken maleness to her and to himself.

Feelings of inadequacy often take the form of jealousy. A jealous person fears that someone is more preferable than he is. The wife says, "I can't hold my man because I am inadequate. I am not pretty enough. I am not sexy enough. I am not sweet enough." The jealous husband says, "I can't hold my wife because I can't buy her enough things. I am not wealthy. I am not handsome. I lack sex appeal. I am a failure." The jealous person feels that he is not capable enough, or lovable enough, or beautiful enough. The things he is jealous about are always externals. In fact, a jealous person's love is based upon externals because jealousy is motivated by the lies of personal deficiency, and these are always negative and of this world. A jealous husband will be envious of another man's good looks, his wealth, or his prestige and status. A jealous wife will be envious of other women's beauty, their wealth, their social position, or their seductiveness. If she has caught her man by seduction, she will be terrified by any other woman who obviously is being successful using that style. She is terrified because she knows with a sure knowledge that her husband is vulnerable to seduction.

Jealousy is often based on feelings of inadequacy. The person who is jealous distrusts himself. And what does he distrust? He distrusts his own inner beauty, his own inner value. He does not believe that he is lovable or capable. He does not know himself. He is so immersed in his layers and defenses and deceptions that he believes he *is* what his substitute world-self proclaims. He has partially lost, or forgotten, or perhaps never known his true identity. He cannot trust, because he cannot really love. And his respect for his "loved" one matches his respect for himself, for he distrusts her even as he distrusts himself.

People who distrust others almost always distrust themselves. A person who is exceedingly jealous or possessive is usually saying through his actions and attitude that he is not self-secure. Were he self-secure and self-confident, he would say, "If she doesn't love me for my true values, for my real self, then I am not interested. If she is happy somewhere else, then that is where I want her to be." True love wants the greatest happiness for the other person. True love has nothing to do with jealousy, revenge, or hostility. These destructive ways of behavior are styles of the substitute self and tools of the devil. They are frustrating and thwarting. Jealousy especially is destructive to the person who employs it and to those unfortunate persons who find they are living with it.

A healthy person can have an affectionate relationship with other people, both male and female, that is not hostile, hateful, possessive, or manipulative. He can relate with both male and female persons in ways that are nonsexual. He loves his neighbors as he purely loves his father, his mother, his brother, or his sister. He does not need to marry everyone he loves. He recognizes that the sexual relationship has a specific function that deals with the family and with family fulfillment. He knows that the sexual exchange is not a personal biological necessity. Neither males nor females need sex for themselves.

Both males and females can live very happily all of their lives without the sexual relationship.

But today, most people do not believe that. Many, many persons have been taught by the world, by society, by rationalizing, needy men and women, that as people get closer and closer they inevitably must end up in bed together. They believe that this is a natural and uncontrollable biological conclusion to any kind of mutual relationship. This deception has been drummed into their heads by Satan and the world until they think they cannot do otherwise. I remember a man who lived by this philosophy. He was otherwise intelligent and learned, with a Ph.D. in chemistry. This man had a daughter who was approaching fourteen and he loved her very much, he had enjoyed many hours with her. He was very honest with me, and one day I opposed his philosophy by saying, "Well, if you love your daughter so much, are you going to take her to bed?"

"Well," he replied, "I'm pretty scared of it sometimes. I am trying to avoid it. I'm not being as affectionate with her as I was when she was younger."

And what did his daughter say? She said, under great emotional pressure, "I think there is something wrong with me. My father doesn't love me anymore. There must be something hateful inside me. I wish I could never grow up. I wish my daddy would hug me again." And she wept as though her heart would break.

False sexuality as a substitute style is a great sickness. What both males and females need to learn is that true love—real, human, family, physical affection—doesn't have to do with sex. True love is an exchange between souls in a treatment that matches the beauty and nobility of each person's spiritual identity. When two souls come together in marriage to create a family, to grow, and to learn and increase their love thereby, the sexual exchange is there to contribute to them and to their union with great majesty and sacred power. But in any other context the sexual union is destructive. Love does not follow sex, nor is love based in sex, nor does love require sex. In fact, the overwhelming majority of human love relationships are not, or ought not to be, sexually oriented at all.

That sex is man's most fundamental and basic need is a lie, compounded by Satan through the world to mislead and distract us from achieving our eternal promise. Learning to love each other truly, purely, without use or guile—learning to love everyone, male or female, old or young, black or white, with a love that may be carried with us when we leave this earth life—this is our opportunity, and indeed our obligation. For how can we claim to have maintained our spiritual identity when we become so easily enslaved to styles and crutches that nourish our negative selves and stifle our spirits? How can we claim to have overcome the world and mastered mortality when we submit ourselves so freely to the world's deceptions and to Satan and his lies and perversions? How can we return to our heavenly parents having lived oblivious to the true love they taught us before we left them? Reality is clear: "They who keep their first estate shall be added upon; and they who keep not their first estate shall not have glory in the same kingdom with those who keep their first estate; and they who keep their second estate shall have glory added upon their heads for ever and ever." (Abraham 3:26.)

The glory that will be ours, if we succeed, will be to have become as our heavenly parents are, like them in character and nature, all loving, all comprehending, all understanding, and consequently, all powerful.

Indeed, this is a challenge and a future well worth our utmost effort.

12

Nourishing the Spirit

And mark this: Every time we have opportunity and fail to live up to that truth which is within us, every time we fail to express a good thought, every time we fail to perform a good act, we weaken ourselves, and make it more difficult to express that thought or perform that act in the future. Every time we perform a good act, every time we express a noble feeling, we make it more easy to perform that act or express that feeling another time. (David O. McKay.)

Therefore, my son, see that you are merciful unto your brethren; deal justly, judge righteously, and do good continually. . . . For that which ye do send out shall return unto you again. (Alma 41:14-15.)

It seems to be an eternal law of our existence that we reap what we sow. Anger begets anger, hostility begets hostility, hate begets hate, and fortunately, laughter also begets laughter, joy begets joy, and love begets love. The things we do rub off on those around us. The kind of person we are influences our neighbors to be that same kind of person. If we are genuinely loving, we do not reap hate, anger, and hostility, and, if we are angry and hostile, we never reap love and sweetness. It is the law of our existence that we reap what we sow, that we have restored to us that which we send out from ourselves.

Keeping our first estate in this life means keeping our spiritual perspective, recognizing our spiritual identity, and maintaining its preeminence over all other things. This is what "overcoming the world" means. Actually, keeping our first estate is our normal position. It is where we ought to be. Keeping our first estate in the midst of our living and experiencing and growing in our second estate is, or ought to be, our primary aim.

Helping the spirit to emerge and grow is like helping any other living thing to emerge and grow. Even as a plant requires appropriate environment and nourishment, so also the spirit needs appropriate environment and nourishment. Barriers inhibiting growth must be removed; the black plastic and the bark mulch must be stripped away so that sunlight and nutrients can flow freely. Thick, muffling defenses and misguiding styles must be recognized and cast off, and nourishment and environment appropriate to the spirit must be provided—an environment like that which we enjoyed before the world was, when we lived with our heavenly parents, when we were nourished by true love and respect without selfishness or guile, where each of us was filled always with a sweet knowledge of who we were and how unutterably great were our purposes. This is the level of living we ought to be seeking. This is the level we are encouraged to create in ourselves and in our loved ones. This is our potential—indeed, our opportunity *and* our necessity. It is not an impossible task, for our Heavenly Father has provided us with the ability within ourselves to accomplish it, and he has provided us with the Holy Ghost to comfort, guide, and help us.

The problem is that most of us do not take advantage of the sources of power and strength and inner nourishment available to us. We are so caught up in the things of the world that we do not choose the better part. We do not choose to overcome the world as we are commanded, but instead, choose to submit to it, allowing it to overcome us. In the process, we submit ourselves to the deceptions of the evil one and become his followers rather than followers of the Lord and Savior Jesus Christ.

Achieving and maintaining spirituality in our mortal lives is the narrow way to which Jesus pointed while he was on earth. When achieved, it encourages godliness and discourages evil. It is easier to love others when we recognize their spiritual identities. It is easier to not abuse ourselves when we are aware of our own spiritual identity. Making a marriage, raising a family, following a profession, doing any righteous thing becomes a more beautiful experience when the spiritual perspective is maintained. Quarreling, contention, competition, jealousy, hate, revenge disappear in the light of the spiritual perspective. Spirituality is the key to keeping our first estate. We should devote ourselves to it, reading the scriptures, praying always, attending our meetings, honoring the priesthood, listening to the living prophet, actively working in our organizations and assignments, in short, doing everything we can to put ourselves in a position where our heavenly natures might continue to grow as they were meant to do.

When the spiritual perspective is the base for all of our thoughts and motivations, love is the kind of action we perform. Real love is spiritual; it is the positive kind of interaction that has always provided nourishment to the soul, both in oneself and in others, in the preexistence and in mortality. The spiritual perspective demands that the aim of all our relationships be providing and attaining this nourishment. Love encourages the spirit self to emerge. It provides the food supply that the spirit self must have to become what it is meant to become, to do the jobs that it is assigned to do.

Accordingly, our major targets must always be eternal targets, and our styles (the ways we reach toward these targets) must always be congruent with spiritual reality. Our interactions with others will be positive, for true love is always positive; it cannot be made negative. True love is self-perpetuating; it builds upon itself. The more one truly loves a person, the more love he has *for* that person—the more he gives, the more he receives. Yet real love cannot be measured or compared; it cannot be described or quantified. Love is an originally available quality of the soul; when it is developed, it is an attained attitude of being.

Real love expresses itself in treatment that matches a person's spiritual identity. One must, therefore, be sensitive, able to perceive another person's identity, in order to love him. Love is based upon knowledge. One cannot love in ignorance. Ignorant, insensitive people cannot love. To really know a human being is to love him; understanding a human being unavoidably yields love.

A student once said to me, "Why do you say that understanding brings love? It seems to me that understanding is merely the means or the avenue by which we react to another person. It seems to me that the more I come to understand the identity of something, the more I am able to decide whether I should love it or hate it."

I replied, "That is exactly right, but in human beings, understanding always leads to love because the real identity of human beings is so very precious, so very beautiful, so very powerful. Understanding opens the eyes of the spirit and allows us to see this. It allows us to see beyond outward appearances. That soul, which at last we perceive, is so overwhelming and wonderful that the more we see of it, the more we are led to love it. But we do have to take the journey down through the layers, past all the phony, counterfeit, substitute things, to understand."

"But," he said, "lots of people say that they understand someone when in reality they hate him."

I replied, "Then they don't really understand that other person. They may comprehend one or two of his particular problems, and they may hate these problems. They may transfer their hate for his action to him. They may say, 'I hate him when he lies to me,' but it is really his lying they hate, not him."

"But his lying keeps them from loving him," he replied.

"Yes, it does. But ultimately they must come to ask what is in his life that makes him lie. How does lying pay off for him? Why does he accept a counterfeit for the truth? To understand a person, one must see beyond his defense systems, his misplaced targets, his substitute styles. When one can pass beyond these, he can begin to know the real person who dwells inside. And to really know another person, that is, to understand him, is to love him. It is unavoidable."

Knowledge is vital to love, as are honesty and sincerity. Of course, such great principles as these can be abused, and often are. And when they are, it is evident that the abuser, either ignorantly or intentionally, has lost his perspective. He either does not or he chooses not to see himself in others. He has rejected the human sympathy necessary to real knowledge and understanding.

In both first and second estates, in preexistence and mortality, the more one knows of himself, the more he *can* know of others—the more one loves and respects himself, the more he is able to love and respect others.

But one must not mistake selfishness for true love of self. Selfishness is a counterfeit and is always defensive. True love of self is based upon understanding oneself, upon knowing oneself. True love of self is self-regard. People who really love themselves are not selfish or proud; they are not arrogant or conceited. Only immature people are this way. Selfishness is childish; it is defensive and shows insecurity. Self-regard is maturity; it is confident and secure. It promotes understanding and service. God's work is never selfish; it is always concerned with others. Spiritual maturity attained is Godhood.

When a person comes to truly love himself, he begins to see himself in others. He finds that what he loves in himself he loves in others. It is a sign of spiritual maturity to recognize that one does indeed love others as he loves himself. It is impossible to love another more than oneself, because real love is measureless. It has no bounds; it cannot be compared.

Real love is made up of many parts, but the two major contributive ones might be called *sameness* and *uniqueness*.

Sameness love is loving yourself in others because all human beings are generally the same. When one looks out over a great field of grass, he sees all the blades of grass together. They seem all the same. They are all green. They all move the same way. They have the same appearance; together, they are one great mass of green. Yet if one takes those blades of grass and puts each one under a microscope, he will find that there is not one exactly like another. Each has unique characteristics. It is so also with human beings. Human beings are the same in general physical appearance. They are the same in general mental attitudes. They are the same in their general emotional needs. Every human being has the same needs for dignity, for positive treatment, for love, respect, and regard. Every human being has the same need to love and be loved. These are the same in all people. Sameness is a foundation for all human love.

Uniqueness, however, is based upon the specialness of each individual. Every person who has ever lived, or who will yet live, has special qualities that are unique with him. Uniqueness love is specific and detailed; it requires closeness, intimacy, and long periods of time, but it produces a depth of relationship that can be obtained in no other way. Deep love relationships are fashioned in uniqueness love. They are based upon internals and are genuine. Such love relationships are of God and are divine; they are the kind of love relationships that we enjoyed in our preexistent first estate.

Deep love relationships require time. Our mortal dimensions limit us so that we achieve very few such deep relationships. Even the most healthy, whole person has time for only a few deep friends. He may have many superficial friends and general acquaintances, but he simply does not have time in his life to learn to know the intricate uniqueness of many individuals. His life will allow only husband or wife, five or six children, and perhaps two or three couples with whom he feels some level of deep relationship. Yet, with these few people, he develops a permanency and a sweetness and an understanding that surpasses all else. The extended closeness of companionship provides knowledge of each person's uniqueness to the point that his interaction with those he loves is based upon a knowledge of their real selves. Achieving such relationships is part of keeping our first estate; it is part of our creating a celestial kingdom for ourselves. It is part of our learning to be the kind of people who may be comfortable where God is.

Uniqueness love is the love every person requires. Uniqueness love is the food that nourishes the spirit and sustains it so that it can emerge and do the jobs assigned to it. All of our interactions with others ought to be directed toward encouraging this spiritual emergence in ourselves and in others.

Our lives are strikingly social. They were meant to be. We are not tested alone. As an aid to our achievement, we are admonished to be kind and noble, to be considerate and understanding, to help and teach our brothers and sisters by faith and by prayer and by sensitive counsel—and we are constantly promised that if we do these things, we not only will succeed in helping others and promoting the kingdom of God, but we ourselves also will grow and change. The Lord has said: "In doing these things thou wilt do the greatest good unto thy fellow beings, and wilt promote the glory of him who is your Lord. Wherefore, be faithful; stand in the office which I have appointed unto you; succor the weak, lift up the hands which hang down, and strengthen the feeble knees. And if thou art faithful unto the end thou shalt have a crown of immortality, and eternal life in the mansions which I have prepared in the house of my Father." (D&C 81:4-6.)

To become fit for eternal life is the great challenge of our second estate. Eternal life is all encompassing. It is unlimited, expanding, powerful. Joy and beauty and unspeakable tenderness and compassion are its realities. But attaining eternal life is not an event like a graduation or an award; it is a process, marked by conscious effort and constant sincere striving.

13

Choosing to Become

When I was a child, I spake as a child, I understood as a child, I thought as a child: but when I became a man, I put away childish things. (1 Corinthians 13:11.)

Could a greater miracle take place than for us to look through each other's eyes for an instant? (Henry David Thoreau.)

Love is a cooperative effort. No man stands alone—or, at least, no man stands as easily alone as he might with the help of others. And there are ways to help each other in this keeping of our first estate. There are ways to help the real self emerge and grow, ways to learn real love, and ways to extend it to each other and accept it in return.

Motivation is the key. Motivation means the moving force behind one's actions. There are always motivations for every choice—social, vocational, moral, financial. Our motivations govern our choice of the clothes we wear, the houses we buy, the friends we have, the interests we have. For instance, why should a woman want to be a schoolteacher? What are the *right* reasons for her to enter upon such a work? She may have many secondary reasons or motivations, such as needing to earn money, or needing to work while her children are in school, or wanting to wield her power over people, but the right reason, the basic primary reason, should be that she feels that through teaching she can most fully express and share her being.

The successful giver of love is full of genuine love and wants to give; he wants to share. This is his reason to interact at all. His motivation is a being motivation; it is a growth motivation. He wants to fulfill his *being*—not his getting, or his having, or his appearing, but his real being. His primary motivation for any choice of action is to express his uniqueness, to grow, to share, to give liberally from his own genuine fullness.

What if one does not have any fullness to give from? What if he is deficient in love? His motivations then are deficiency motivations. The love he has is made up of substitutes—possessiveness, exclusiveness, control, use—cheap substitutes that he has come to accept as the genuine article. Because he is really deficient, he is always looking for love; and because he has mutated, he seldom recognizes it or accepts it when it appears. He desires only to fill his deficiency with more cheap substitutes. This is what is really happening when a person seeking love says: "You don't love me because you also love others. If you really loved me, I would be your only love." Or "You don't love me because you will not come over here at three o'clock in the morning when I call." Or "You don't love me because you won't give me money to buy what I want." Or "You don't love me because you won't do things for me. You won't serve me. You won't let me use you." Such people are selfish; they are inconsiderate; they are childish. Such people are primarily concerned with getting, having, controlling, appearing. They know very little about being.

How important it is to be able to know our real motivations! If, in our interactions with other people, we are mostly concerned about getting something for ourselves, seeking to fill up some deficiency inside us, whatever it may be, then most probably, we are seeking love substitutes. However, if we are mostly concerned with really sharing from our unique and genuine fullness, then we are involved with real love.

But the interaction concerns a receiver also. The successful receiver has the same intent as the successful giver—that is, to share. The receiver likes to receive love, but he doesn't *need* to. He is not in a desperate situation. He knows what love is. He recognizes the essential sameness of all humanity, and yet he knows also their essential uniqueness. He receives love comfortably. When he is told that he is loved or liked, or when he is complimented, he feels more human. He feels more lovable and capable; he feels more humble, more beautiful. He accepts genuine positive treatment because that matches his spiritual identity.

On the other hand, the deficient receiver does not receive love comfortably. When love is given to him or when compliments are extended, he receives them negatively. The mother says to her daughter, "I really love you, Jane." And the daughter answers, "Well, you're supposed to. You're my mother, aren't you?" The husband says to the wife, "I really love you. You're a good wife to me." And the wife replies, "No, I'm not. You're just saying that because you want me to be happy." The therapist says to his patient, "I really like you, Tom." And Tom answers, "You're supposed to. You're my psychologist. You like me because that's what I'm paying you to do." The teacher says to the student, "You surely did well on that test. I was very pleased with your work. You got an A." The student replies, "Oh, I just lucked out. I'm really not that smart," or "The test was no good. You should give harder tests." This kind of a receiver always does something to twist the love that is extended so that he may stay negative. His aim is to reinforce his negative self.

Why does he do this? He does it because he has mutated to the point that his negative, substitute self *is*, to him, his identity. Negativism has become his love supply; he does not feel lovable, capable, humble, or beautiful. He twists positive things around so that they become negatives for him. He says to himself, "No one can really love me. They only act like they love me because they have to." Or he says, "I wonder what it is that he wants from me." In every interaction he sees some other motive. He finds it very difficult to accept real love. "That's not real love," he says. "If you really loved me, you'd give me what *I* want." He sticks to his own definitions, and his definitions always imply that his identity is negative.

In deficiency motivation, both giver and receiver give and receive in order to get. This is false nurturance. Their success becomes a condition of their personal worth. They say, "I will be your father, your mother, your teacher, your scoutmaster, your doctor, your nurse. I will help you to achieve certain goals if you will do what I say." But behind their words is the unspoken message, "When you achieve these goals, then you will be nurturing me. I will feel good about myself. Your behavior is my crutch." Such people have their worth tied to the appearances, or performances, of other people. They give in order to get. They give in order to fill up their own deficiencies.

Now, action that fills a deficiency may not be wrong; in fact, it is the way that deficient people can become well. However, it is necessary that they learn to fill their deficiency with *real* love supplies. They must learn to differentiate between genuine love and the counterfeits that they have been accepting. Loving people who want to help will need to say again and again, "I will not do the things you demand, because you are too precious to be treated like that." Through good and loving firmness, the deficient person will finally learn that there are people who will not deal in substitutes, who will not be shaken from their own self-respect, who will not abuse themselves by allowing themselves or others to be misused.

It is so easy to do right things for wrong reasons. Parents, teachers, youth leaders so often compromise themselves in order to be popular with their children or their charges, being overly permissive in order to gain allegiance. They feel that they are being very successful with their responsibility, but in reality, their purpose has moved from directing and inspiring right conduct to filling their own selfish ego needs. The result is the exact reverse of what they have intended, for their example is one of wrong conduct, and their parenthood or leadership is acceptable only as long as their children or followers approve.

The Spirit of the Lord is never found in deficiency love. God's love proceeds from a fullness. His love is *being* love. It is this kind of love that we must learn if we want to become as he is. This is the perspective that Alma taught the saints beside the waters of Mormon before their baptism. He told them they should be "willing to bear one another's burdens, that they may be light . . . willing to mourn with those that mourn; yea, and comfort those that stand in need of comfort, and to stand as witnesses of God at all times and in all things, and in all places . . . even until death, that ye may be redeemed of God, and be numbered with those of the first resurrection, that ye may have eternal life." (Mosiah 18:8-9.)

Alma told them that they must remember who they are, that as children of God they must genuinely love one another through mortality, especially in witnessing and strengthening each other in the reality of their relationship to the Lord. Alma committed the saints to know one another and to understand one another so that real love might be a possibility for them, so that thereby they might grow to be like God, fit to be redeemed and able to enjoy eternal life.

It is so, too, with each one of us. We must commit ourselves to obtain this kind of love relationship. We must learn to be genuine givers and receivers.

But to do this, we must analyze ourselves—our targets, our styles, and the payoffs that these bring. We must ask ourselves what our favorite love supplies are and compare these with what might make us feel more lovable, more capable, more precious, more beautiful, more human.

It is interesting to examine our favorite love supplies through our lives. The progress moves generally from surface to depth as one grows older. Physical affection is a constant, appearing at all ages and all depths, but alongside this, children and young people name things: money, cars, physical appearance, compliments. Middle-aged persons name security, reputation, social acceptance. Older people name integrity, respect, regard, knowledge, understanding. Age and maturity and experience seem to bring recognition at last of man's inherent spiritual need to be understood and to understand others.

Understanding implies an ability to enter into somebody else's feeling world, to see through his eyes, to hear through his ears, to feel what he feels. Genuine understanding urges expression, assurance, companionship. Such an understanding is called *empathy*. Empathy is proof of our presence. In the internal life of another person, it is the proof of our caring.

Empathy is the most valuable of all skills in breaking through the muffling, restricting layers that keep the spirit self from emerging. Empathy must be practiced to be mastered. There are steps to its achievement. Some of these steps require only a split second, yet each step has its place and its importance. In time, as empathy becomes an integral part of one's style of interaction with others, these steps become automatic. They merge together smoothly without differentiation.

The first step is to establish confidence with the other person. This requires listening, with ears, with eyes, with feelings. Voice tone, body posture, facial expression, words, all these reveal how the inside self is reacting. To achieve genuine empathy, you must listen with your heart; you must allow the other person to feel safe and secure in your presence. People are like castles, with deep moats and heavy drawbridges. Only the person inside the castle lowers the drawbridge to let others in. If the drawbridge is not lowered, you will not be able to go inside. You must listen and feel with him so that he feels secure with you and allows you to come inside his castle to gather information, for you must know not only what has happened, but also how he feels about what has happened.

The second step is to take the information that you have gathered and sort through your own feelings to see if you have ever had any of these kinds of experiences. Everyone has a storehouse of feelings, but some people's storehouses are more full than others. Sensitive people, who are aware of what is happening in their lives, automatically store their feelings, their life experiences, for future reference. They have excellent memories and are not afraid to remember. Life, to them, is a great and thrilling experience, to be constantly relived and enjoyed. People who have learned, for one reason or another, to shut out feelings and experiences have a hard time achieving empathy. People like Harry's wife, who could not tell the difference between arguing and discussing, find that when they begin to search into their feeling storehouse, they are empty; they have no perceptions or interpretations to draw upon. They cannot understand other people's feelings because they have no points of reference. They cannot judge how others feel because they have no evaluated experience in their storehouse to draw upon.

One needs to be a sensitive person to understand other people's feelings. Now, this does not mean that one has to have had a physical experience exactly like that had by another person. It means only that one needs to realize his feelings. For instance, if a murderer is telling you how he felt when he murdered someone, you don't have to have murdered someone to know how he feels. If you gather your information carefully, you will find that underneath the physical act of murder, there is either intense anger or intense fear. This feeling is the feeling you are after, for most people have felt anger or fear on an intense level. Your feeling can be drawn upon to create empathetic understanding, even of a murderer.

But some people are pretty tightly closed up. They have suppressed and repressed their feelings, especially their intense feelings, all their lives. These kinds of people have a very difficult time achieving empathy. I once worked with a group of prison guards. We were discussing empathy. Suddenly one attendant said, "Oh, well, we have heard about empathy for ten years. Why don't you tell us something new? We know empathy real good."

I said, "Well, you come up to the front here, and I'll be someone with some worried feelings. I'll tell you about these feelings and you demonstrate empathy."

"Right on," he says.

So he walked up by me and stood there and waited. I looked

out the window and it was snowing outside, great big flakes of
snow. The freeway was just outside the prison wall. I had come
up this freeway that morning in the snow. The road had been
very bad and was now becoming even worse. I was worried
about getting home. As I looked out the window, I said to him,
"I'm really worried about how I'm going to get home tonight.
This morning the freeway was quite bad, and this afternoon it's
even worse. Look outside now—it's five-thirty and there's a lot
of traffic. How am I going to get home? My wife and my kids are
alone and waiting for me. I'm really worried." I looked at him
in a worried way and raised my hands helplessly, waiting for
him to help me out.

But he didn't say anything.

I repeated again. "I'm really worried about getting home to
my wife and my children." And I let my voice drop softly.

He stood there quite a while, then finally said in an off-
hand manner, "Did you drive up to the prison by yourself or
with somebody else?"

I answered, "Well, I came up with somebody else, but don't
you see how I feel? I'm worried."

He missed it completely. He said nothing at all. He just
stood there.

I tried again. "You see, I'm really nervous about not being
able to get home. It's snowing out there, and I saw thirteen cars
off the freeway on my way to the prison this morning. I'm upset
about getting home." And then I added, "Do you see how I
feel?"

But he just stood and scratched his head and finally said,
"Well, how far away from the prison do you live?"

I replied, "It's about sixty-five or seventy miles. Do you see
how I feel?"

He looked at me, puzzled, and said, "Well?"

So I told him the whole thing over again, how frightened I
was and how I might not get home safely. Then I waited.

Finally he replied, "Well, do you have somebody in town
you can stay with overnight?"

I said, "I don't want to stay here overnight. I want to go

home. My wife and kids are expecting me. Don't you see how I feel?"

He looked at me dumbly, and finally, in complete exasperation, he raised both his hands in the air and almost shouted at me, "Well, I didn't make it snow."

Now this prison guard did not achieve empathy. He not only was unable to listen and gather the information he needed for an empathic response, but he also was unable to find any experience in his own storehouse to use as reference points for understanding how worried I was. The only path of action he could find was to try to solve my problem. And even though he meant well, solving my problem was not empathy. I didn't want him to solve my problem; I intended to solve that myself. I wanted understanding. I wanted to know that I was not alone, that someone out there understood how I felt. But instead of giving me the understanding and the comfort I sought, he provided substitutes, solutions, explanations: perhaps some other driver would drive me home, perhaps I could stay here instead of going home at all. In frustration he questioned whether I had any right to feel the way I felt and to burden him with my feelings. His reactions were far from empathy.

Solving another person's problem may be evidence of concern, but it is not empathy. All that guard had to say to me was, "You look awfully tense. You're worried, aren't you. You're worried that you'll not get home." And that would have told me that he understood how I felt. I probably would have replied, "Yes, I made it up here this morning. I don't know how. But I'll probably be able to make it home." Assurance and understanding were what I needed. Companionship and confidence were what I was asking for. I would have received it had he been able to feel my feelings.

The key to step number two is to ask yourself, "How would I have to feel to say something like that? How would I have to feel to be that disappointed, that hurt, that lost, that lonely, that angry?" Then, equipped with that question, you would need to dive down into your memory storehouse, sort out your feelings, and find a reference feeling inside yourself that would help you to truly understand.

The third step is to let the person know that you understand. Having found a reference point in your own feelings, you are able to put yourself into his position. But care must be taken in letting him know that you understand, for if you say the wrong things, if you are merely polite and really untrue, he may draw up his drawbridge and shut you out of his castle. If you truly have found a reference feeling in your storehouse, what you say to him will ring true. He will accept your love and concern and will derive strength from it.

If, however, you are only acting empathy, what you say will be mere paraphrasing. Paraphrasing is when one simply repeats in his own words what has been said to him. Paraphrasing is not true empathy. It may be an elementary start, but unless there is sincere feeling behind the words, they will sound false and artificial, and the effort will be ineffectual, perhaps even harmful.

I remember trying to learn this great skill, trying to master these principles that they might flow freely. I was training with a young university student who was very bright. During the first twenty minutes of our interview, I tried very hard to paraphrase empathetically, but it was not sincere. Suddenly he stopped and said, "What's wrong with the way I say how I feel?" I was very embarrassed, for I had been caught acting. Even though I was sincerely striving to act out empathy, my sincerity was not enough. Empathy cannot be acted; it must be real.

The fourth step is purely mechanical. It is simply remembering to take turns as you interact. In any conversation between two people, one person must listen while the other talks. The human mind can perform only one operation at one time. It is impossible to both talk and listen. People who interrupt, who talk over another person, never achieve empathy. They don't know how to take turns. Parents often abuse this rule. They teach disrespect. They interrupt their children. They will not allow them to say what they have to say; they steal their children's turns to talk because they are big and can do so. As the years go by, they often wonder why their children have become so selfish, why they won't take turns with other children, why they always cut in and interrupt. Often, they will punish a child for interrupting, never realizing that they have taught it to the child themselves.

People who are more secure in themselves, who understand themselves fairly well, do not interrupt. They have no need to contend or push themselves over someone else's need. They already feel self-sufficient. They can wait for their turn.

Empathy requires this kind of security. As one listens carefully to what another person is saying, searching deep in his own feeling storehouse for a companion experience, he must watch for signals that tell him that it's his turn to speak, his turn to let the other person know that he understands. Until those signals come, he should be very careful to only listen. He may agree and encourage, but he must not interrupt the flow of information.

The signals are plain to see. Usually the speaker's voice will drop, becoming softer. Often the person will seek assurance by saying, "Do you know what I mean? Do you see how I feel?" Or even "What do you think?" Sometimes a person will do something with his eyes or with his face to show you that he wants to switch places, that it's your turn to speak and his turn to listen. But the person who listens must be very sensitive, for often signals are false. A person who is very disturbed and in great need of empathy is under tension. Often he does not know how to take turns himself. The signals may come and you may begin to give the assurance that is empathetic, but the other person may not even listen to you. He may begin to talk again just as though you weren't even there. This is your sign that this signal was false. You are not yet supposed to switch places. You must go back to listening. Relax. Look into his eyes. Encourage him with sincere questions and assurances. Your task is to gather information so that you can genuinely understand. You must not say such things as, "Well my mother does the same thing," or "Why, yesterday I had the same experience." Such statements not only belittle the person's experience (which to him is a singular and peculiar thing), but they also attempt to take over the troubled person's turn. He came to you to tell you his feelings. When you take his turn, he feels stifled. He finds himself more tense and frustrated than he was to start with.

Empathy is difficult to achieve, even when one understands the process and really strives to use it. Once my daughter and I were driving home along the freeway. She was telling me that she wanted to go somewhere to do something, but I had already decided that she should not go. I said, "No, you cannot go. There's no need for you to go." And I wouldn't even listen to her. It was doubly bad because we were on the way home from a lecture where I had been talking about empathy!

At last, she said, "Just a minute now, Dad. Let me tell you *where* I want to go, *what* I want to do, and *why* I want to do it, and will you please be still until I get through."

I had to be careful not to be offended at her frankness. But I decided I should listen, and when she said, "Is that all right?" I said I'd really try. So she started out giving me information, where she was going and why she wanted to go there, reason number one, reason number two, reason number three—and she went on about twenty miles down the freeway. Finally she brought up one reason that really disturbed me, and I said, "Well, that one doesn't even count."

She replied quickly, "Just a minute, Daddy. I'm not through."

I couldn't even be quiet and let her talk for twenty minutes! I couldn't even let her present her case! I thought to myself, Why are you so impatient? Then I realized that I wasn't really listening to her to gather information. Not at all. What I was really doing was getting ready for debate. I was girding myself for the coming argument. I had no empathy at all. It was no wonder we couldn't communicate.

We all do this, especially in our parent-child relationships. It is very difficult for parents to allow their children to become adults, to be treated as adults. It becomes exceedingly difficult when the situation is emotionally threatening because this calls up defenses and triggers substitute styles. It is easy to become involved in substitute programs (such as negating, or solving the problem, or taking away the other person's free agency, or topping his story, fighting with him, arguing with him, defending, accusing, lying, contending, name calling, and so on), when often all he is asking for is merely to be understood. Empathy is not a way of solving another person's problems. It is a way to bolster others so that they can solve their own problems.

Every man must live his life for himself. There is no substitute for one's own experience. Each man must face his own life and deal with it. Each man must decide the kind of person he will be, the kinds of nourishment he will seek for himself, the kinds of payoffs he will accept. This is his test, his experience with mortality, his opportunity to show that he can keep his first estate within his second estate and grow and change and become Christlike, the kind of person who can be happy where God is.

The program is complete and whole and beautiful. It is called the gospel of Jesus Christ. It is very purposefully designed to guide us to a success beyond our presently conceivable, brightest dreams. We cannot fathom the happiness, the fullness, the complete wholeness that await us if we will obey the Savior's directions and meet his requirements. "For if you will that I give unto you a place in the celestial world, you must prepare yourselves by doing the things which I have commanded you and required of you." (D&C 78:7.)

His commands and requirements are not for his benefit, but for ours. They direct us to follow his example and become like him, not only superficially, in words and deeds, but authentically, in our inside hearts and private minds, in our very souls and our very beings. In this way, and in this way only, will we be able to possess and finally encompass eternal life.

There is no other way.

14

Sanctify Yourselves

God has placed in us a pure spirit; when this reigns pre-dominant, without let or hindrance, and triumphs over the flesh and rules and governs and controls as the Lord controls the heavens and the earth, this I call the blessing of sanctification. (Brigham Young.)

But this much I can tell you, that if ye do not watch your-selves, and your thoughts, and your words, and your deeds, and observe the commandments of God . . . even unto the end of your lives, ye must perish. And now, O man, remember, and perish not. (Mosiah 4:30.)

King Benjamin is very brief in the above quotation from Mosiah, but he is speaking an undeniable truth. He is saying that we are responsible not only for our deeds and our words, but also for the very thoughts that produce them. He is saying that we must control our thoughts even as we control our words and our deeds. The measuring rod, he says, is the command-ments of God. If we obey God's commandments, as we have been directed to do, in spirit and thought as well as in deed, we will become sanctified and attain eternal life, but if we do not, we will perish.

Perish means to die. Obviously, since all men must die according to the flesh, King Benjamin is speaking of more than this, for mortal death is not ordinarily dependent upon the criteria he mentions. What he is saying is that we are responsible for governing and directing our internal beings, our minds and our hearts, so that we will sincerely become like our heavenly parents. Failure to do so, he says, will mean that we will die as to the things of Godhood, the great eternal things of truth and right and wondrous beauty and power.

But we were not meant to so perish. Means and materials, enough and to spare, have been amply provided for us in our lives. Supplies of love, the most essential of all our needs, are readily available on every side, from loved ones, friends, neighbors, even remote strangers. Prophets across space and time point the way and warn of error. Revelation from the Lord is readily ours by right of our divine kinship; indeed, we are equipped by our heavenly identity to know truth constantly, beyond our mortal senses. By seeking, we can obtain an insight, a vision, really, of our true spiritual character. And we can derive great strength from this vision, for it is a readily available love supply from ourselves, and meant to be so.

Often, as we define our needs and our potentials, we forget to include a love supply from ourselves. It never occurs to us that this glorious heavenly being, which we really are, can provide us with strength and assurance. We rarely hear of obtaining and using such love supplies. But it is possible and very practical. Love, by its very nature, is self-perpetuating. It feeds on its own fruits: kindness, service, companionship, firmness, appreciation, regard.

Love supplies from the real self begin when we perceive in ourselves a character trait that is evidence of our spirit, such as gentleness, courage, sensitivity, persistence, or sacrifice, a quality of being not taught to us by anyone, although it may have been reinforced over the years by real love.

We must be wary, however, in our inner searching, for outward appearances and performances can be insincere. They may not be what they appear to be. Satan is very adept at producing counterfeit forms. For instance, some people appear to be truly sacrificing, or truly gentle and kind, but their motivations may be to get recognition, praise, or love, or even money or material goods, rather than to express their being. Getting is always a deficiency motivation. When we feel un-comfortable, strange, or suspicious about someone's giving, someone's gentleness, or even our own gentleness, loyalty, or sacrifice, we can know that motivations may not be pure. Our real self thrives on truth and sincerity. It is offended by deceit. It cannot lie. If we will allow it, it will be a private Urim and Thummim for each of us whereby all truth may be made manifest to us.

Now when people obtain a vision of even one character trait that belongs to them, to that heavenly being that is really them, they begin to grow. When they perceive that there really is something inside them that does not come from any culture or environment or from anybody else's personality, something that is evidence of their heavenly being, they begin to be free, for they own something that is utterly independent of the world and its dimensions. No one can ever steal it or take it. No one else has any power over it. No prison door can shut it away. No success or failure can ruin it. It is unique and independent. The knowledge of it lifts them above criticism, above discourage-ment, above failure. It strengthens them in their self-regard. It increases their understanding. It nourishes their sensitivity. And, as the veil opens further for them, as it may do, they discover more about their real selves; inspiration becomes more easily available to them, for the things of the spirit are always discerned by the spirit.

Using the spirit self as a source of love supply comes more easily to one who has received genuine love in his early years from father, mother, and family, teachers, and friends. The spirit's inherent ability to provide love increases as it is consis-tently nourished. As it gains more experience, it becomes more independent and free. A healthy dependency as a child always leads to a healthy independency as an adult.

It is this kind of attained independent security and confidence that makes genuine love possible. A person who achieves this great freedom will be able to love others as the Savior does.

But how to obtain this first flash of vision? The Lord has said that if we will seek, we will find; if we will knock, the door will be opened to us. And it is so. Most people, through sincere prayer and intense self-examination, are able to identify something about themselves that they can acknowledge as a property of their unique spirit self, a true trait of their own heavenly being. They can see, for instance, that they do care deeply about somebody, that they can really feel how other people feel, that they are indeed courageous, loyal, or persistent in overcoming difficulties and failures.

It is thrilling and wonderful to see this realization come to people. "It's me!" they cry out, as though meeting again some lost loved one whom they had not seen for a lifetime. And it really is so, for this glimpse of recognition is a parting of a veil grown impenetrable over the years. It is a vision of realities long forgotten.

But one must not stop there. This break through the muffling layers can open the way to a vast hidden reserve of love, respect, and confidence available within the spirit self. But this requires conscious effort. The person must focus his thoughts upon his new insight. He must strive to realize how valuable and beautiful this newly discovered trait is—that it is real and truly his, and that it is an original-self trait, a true characteristic of his own unique heavenly being. Gradually he will begin to feel a quiet, gentle glow of confidence and security flowing deep inside himself. This is the tiny beginning of a great steady flow of strength available to each of us.

I have seen many people catch this inward vision and sense this inward strength. It is always a positive, deeply moving experience. It cannot be negative because it can never be used to take or to get. It is individual and sacred. "That *is* me, the *real* me!" they exclaim, and they love the vision, the narrow glimpse of the powerful, beautiful being that they really are.

Catching this vision, fleeting though it may be, is very

encouraging. It is available to all of us if we will put ourselves in a position to receive it. However, it requires thoughtful concentration, quiet meditation, honest self-examination, sensitive evaluation. For many of us this may be difficult; we are so cluttered by false defenses that we find it hard to be honest even with ourselves. We are somehow ashamed to search out our own virtues.

To help people with this, we often do what is called "a love circle." This is helpful in group therapy and works well also in a family group, for family home evenings, for instance. Here is the way we do it. Each person in the circle will relate, to the person who is trying to find out what his real self is like, some positive thing that he has felt or glimpsed of that person's true character. As the person being helped hears each person around the circle speak in turn of his strengths and virtues, he begins to see that there are things inside him that he can truly own. He begins to gain confidence and assurance. If he is ready and the timing is right, he may begin to see what the others see; he may begin to see himself.

In families, it is important that everyone in the circle be helped and that everyone participate. Each family member should have opportunity to hear all the other family members tell him what they love about him, expressing something beautiful they have noticed about him, some admirable trait they have seen that is specifically his. They must try not to make it a light-minded game, or a deficiency motivated performance. Comments must be sincere and true; they must never be false or manipulative. Love circles in a family, if correctly done, always increase closeness and bring love such as some families have never seen before. The memory of that revealed closeness, that sweet acceptance and understanding, will last for many months in the family. It will last forever in individual memories.

I have asked persons who have just been in a love circle, "What did the others say about you?" (It is very important to ask about it, for it causes review and contemplation.) Almost without fail they will remember almost every trait mentioned about them. But when I have said to them, "Which of all these things that others see in you do you feel you actually own," they seldom accept them all. The reason for their hesitation is because they sense that perhaps the people in the group don't know the difference between a genuine character trait and a phony one, that perhaps they themselves may not be authentic. Nevertheless, a person can usually accept something from the group's conceptions, something that seems psychologically safe for him to admit as his. When he acknowledges that this accepted trait is present in him, then he begins to own it. He can focus on it, examine it, and recognize how really beautiful it is. In time it will prove to be a precious jewel that he can take out and look at anytime he wants, and he will find that he can receive constant strength and nourishment from it.

No one's spiritual character in mortality is fully perfected. Always, in each of us, there are weaknesses where our potential is underdeveloped or perhaps not developed at all. In every place where there is such weakness, where there is a genuine trait not developed, there will be a large love substitute doing its job.

Love substitutes from ourselves take the form of cheap payoffs derived from thinking certain thoughts. These thoughts produce a feeling, a reaction that is a counterfeit of the genuine feeling we really seek. Most people begin accepting these kinds of love substitutes when they are very young. Parents and others set the example, indulging themselves in thoughts that rewarded them and that were perceivable by others around them. For instance, a mother might think (and show) that because she keeps a clean house she is a better woman than her neighbor. Or a father may think (and show) that because he is educated or belongs to a certain club or group he is superior to others. People often get strength to tolerate extreme rejection and misery by thinking such thoughts. "Well," they say, "I'm the only one that's right. I'm the only one who cares." Or "I'm the one who does the work around here." These are superiority thoughts. They come close to being martyr thoughts, poor-me thoughts, see-me-suffer thoughts. In these thought patterns, a person paints his own portrait as he wants it to be and gets comfort thereby. He accepts this self-induced substitute comfort in the place of the real love that he really needs.

The process is prevalent and common. It can be seen in every form of psychopathology, from schizophrenic anxieties, escapes, and fantasies, through drug addiction, alcoholism, criminality, and prostitution, to complete sociopathic mutation. It is aided on all levels by poor art, sentimental literature, sensational novels, cheap drama, low-minded tasteless films and TV shows, pulp magazines, trashy newspapers, and pornography in all its varied forms.

Thoughts always precede deeds. All forms of neuroses, major and minor—shyness, overweight, temper tantrums, running away—every kind of psychotic problem has some form of thought reward, or fantasy payoff, before it progresses into act and deed. There is always a preliminary psychic discharge that satisfies temporarily, depending upon the depth and intensity of the need. However, as the need increases in intensity, the thought payoff does not satisfy; ultimately, it requires reinforcement with words, and finally deeds.

This works efficiently both positively and negatively. The body is the key. The body is a major reason for our earth life, and it is the means to our degradation or our sanctification. That is why it is so important to have a body—we cannot become celestial without it. In union and harmony with the spirit, the body creates a celestial soul; in opposition to the spirit, it creates a devil.

Through the body, exaltation and degradation are nourished in each one of us. The parts of the body are the nourishers: the brain, the heart, the mouth, the hands, arms, legs, feet—each encourages each. Positive thoughts in the brain, welcomed, multiplied, made permanent and comfortable, and finally owned, create positive feelings in the heart, feelings that in turn are expressed by the mouth in positive words and that are acted out in positive deeds by the hands, the arms, the legs, the feet—all of these nourish and strengthen the spirit, thereby keeping and consolidating both first and second estates. Likewise, negative thoughts, welcomed and repeated in the brain until finally owned, breed negative feelings in the heart, feelings that in turn produce negative words in the mouth and that are enacted in deeds done by the hands, or the arms, or other parts of the body—nourishing and strengthening the negative self, voiding the first estate and losing the glorious potential of the second.

This is why it is so important that we be sensitive to the workings of our thoughts. We need to be aware of the kinds of thoughts we think. We need to ask ourselves, "How did these thoughts get into my mind? Where did they come from?" And later, "When did these thoughts first become acceptable? How did they pay off then? And how do they work now, with my spouse and my children?" Often we can detect which of our thought patterns are deficiency motivated, and perhaps even discover and remedy the deficiency that is encouraging them. The key for judgment is the degree to which our thoughts match reality, especially the reality of our heavenly identification. Thoughts that match this reality are not counterfeits, but are from our inner selves. These thoughts should be honored and nourished. But thoughts that do not match this reality are love substitutes and should be rejected and cast out.

We need to work to get along with our thoughts even as we work to get along with other people. The principles are the same: *empathy*, to listen, to understand, to be sensitive to ourselves; *openness*, to be aware of our feelings, to contemplate them honestly; and *firmness*, to respect ourselves enough to insist on "being" relationships.

The first step in controlling thoughts is not to ignore them or to suppress them, but to notice them and to identify which self is promoting them, the false, negative self or the real, positive self. We can recognize this by assessing the thought's content and the feeling it brings to us. What kind of a thought is it, and does it make us feel good about ourselves? Does it bring us peace, self-confidence, esteem, respect—the things that match our true identity? Or does it mislead us, upset us, debase and belittle us?

It requires accurate empathy and absolute honesty to sort out our thought patterns according to their sources and targets. It takes a great deal of understanding and openness to be able to identify which self is talking when we are thinking, and why. Yet this must be done, for we cannot control what we do not understand. Thoughts that compensate for some deficiency in us obviously come from our negative self, as do those thoughts that are directly negative, that express in some way that we are incapable or unlovable. More difficult, however, to detect and classify are those negative thoughts that appear to be positive— selfish sacrifice, false generosity, self negation, false nurturance, supermothering, spoiling, pleasing, over-achieving—compensation thought patterns that come from the negative self even though they appear at first to be positive and good.

The second step in controlling our thoughts is to discard those thoughts that are from the negative self. This requires firmness and persistence. It is not easy. One must be careful not to drift into repressing or suppressing these thoughts instead of discarding them. Repression and suppression are lies and of Satan. When we repress or suppress our thoughts, we actually deny that we have them; we stuff them down deep under our layers of clutter and ignore that they are there, hiding them so that we cannot understand or control them. There, hidden away, they ferment and breed, producing the psychosomatic illnesses—depression, insomnia, ulcers, and so on—that inevitably follow dishonesty in ourselves.

It requires true emotional independence to discard thoughts. One must be able honestly and firmly to say, "I am independent of other people in these thoughts. I can throw them out because I made them up in the first place. I may have seen similar thoughts in others, but my thoughts are mine. I chose to have them. I am in charge of all the thoughts I think, and therefore I can throw out what I will. I do not need to hide them or store them, nor do I need to lie to myself about having them." Recognition, acknowledgment, and firmness, these are keys to putting negative thoughts out of our minds.

The third step is to reinforce our positive thoughts. We need to set up a plan to give our positive self equal time—more than equal time. We need to hear more often from our real selves and less often from our counterfeit, negative selves. We need to expose our negative self for what it is: unreal, counterfeit, false. We need to realize how silly it is and then throw it and its substitute inspirations away.

We need to discipline ourselves to obey the thoughts that come from our positive being, to reinforce our insight and position by singing positive songs or inspirational hymns, or memorizing positive verses and sayings. We may need to force ourselves to look for the good in others as well as in ourselves, and to avoid false praise and all manner of dishonesty. Consciously and deliberately, we must fill our minds with positive thoughts, not as a cover for our satanic negative self, but as a true expression of our own glorious heavenly being. The Lord has said:

"Let virtue garnish thy thoughts unceasingly; then shall thy confidence wax strong in the presence of God; and the doctrine of the priesthood shall distil upon thy soul as the dews from heaven.

"The Holy Ghost shall be thy constant companion, and thy scepter an unchanging scepter of righteousness and truth; and thy dominion shall be an everlasting dominion, and without compulsory means it shall flow unto thee forever and ever." (D&C 121:45-46.)

The result of correctly using the vast love supply inherent in ourselves is to become independent and free, even as our heavenly parents have become. It is to succeed in life. It is to keep our first estate and our second estate. It is, as King Benjamin implied, not to perish, but to achieve exaltation and eternal life.

What more magnificent promise could there be than this?

Afterword

All things unto me are spiritual. (D&C 29:34.)

A few mornings ago, very early, just as day began to light our bedroom, my wife and I were awakened by our littlest boy. He came wide awake into our bedroom, nudging us, whispering in our ears, wanting to come into our bed with us. I was grumpy and half asleep. But I made room for him, grumping sleepily at him to try to hold still. He climbed in between us, curled himself up close beside me, and began to try.

But his feet wouldn't cooperate. They began to wiggle together against me somehow—and then his knees—and pretty soon he had his arms over my shoulders and his hot cheek against my back. I finally rolled over, mumbling, "Can't you hold still? What are you trying to do?"

My little boy looked at me. His eyes shone dark bright even in the dull morning, and puzzlement was in them. He reached for my cheek. "I was just loving you, Dad," he said. "I was just loving you."

I lay there ashamed. How selfish I was! How unwilling to share, to give and receive! What kind of a father, or teacher, or person was I anyway, to forget so easily who I was, and who others were, and how deep and real our needs are? "In that body dwells a heavenly being," a prophet had said. I looked at my little son. His hand still touched my cheek, and his face was close to mine at the edge of the big pillow. "You were loving me," I said, gaining time.

"Oh yes, Daddy," he whispered, "always and always," and he began to wiggle all over with the joy of it like a small puppy in the arms of his master.

It was a good lesson. I needed it. My little boy, less influenced by the world and its counterfeits, had come to me without guile, had come for an exchange of love and assurance in the early morning light, wanting to share his unbounded fullness without restriction or condition. And I had chosen sleep in its place! How limited we are in our insight, and how quick we are to forget.

Later on, as the day passed, I found myself thinking often of my little boy and of his identity as a child of God, a powerful, intelligent, heavenly being dwelling for a few preparatory years in a little body, and lent to me briefly to lead and guide and walk beside. I looked about me and saw my world filled with people like him—sons and daughters, fathers and mothers, brothers and sisters, each one a bright and shining spirit child of heavenly parents, each one striving, needing, wanting, hoping—trying to make his way through this great second estate, learning, and growing, and becoming. How right it is, I thought, that our mortal experience builds upon our premortal experience. "Remember who you are," my father had said. It was the key to everything.

All we have to do is do it, and constantly. In the morning when our loved ones come for love, we need to remember who they are; at midday, when the demands of business and profession press worldly hard upon us, we need to remember who we are; in the evening, with family and friends, at table or entertainment, we need to remember what our purposes really are and why we are alive in this dimension of time and space. Everything follows this remembering—sensitivity, honesty, confidence, respect, worth, capability, lovability, empathy, and all the vast awareness of patterns and styles of needs and behaviors, authentic and substitute—all the facts of true human freedom and temporal and eternal happiness, all of these and more enter into our lives by this great key.

It is a constant battle to keep that perspective. Remembering our spiritual identity, keeping our first estate, is *the* crucial battle of our mortal life. Entering that battle, and winning, means eternal victory.

But some of us never get around to it. We live always in the preparation. We like to know about things; we like to read about them, to talk about them, even to study them or make a profession out of investigating them, but we never get around to really practicing them, to making them integral parts of our everyday lives. We shun the battle. We are procrastinators; we never quite come to actuality. Oh, we mean to. We always mean to, and we prolong our girding for the battle until we finally fool ourselves into thinking that our girding *is* the battle, and that we have fought our fight and done our bit simply by investigating, discussing, and proclaiming our position and our intent.

It always reminds me of the biblical account of Ben-hadad, king of Syria, who swelled up before Ahab, king of Israel, and forced him to unwilling conflict.

"Thy silver and thy gold are mine!" Ben-hadad shouted. Then he shook his fist and strutted, "Thy wives also and thy children—are mine!"

And Ahab, wicked to the ways of God but wise in the ways of the world, muttered back at him an unending truth, "Let not him that girdeth on his harness boast himself as he that putteth it off." (1 Kings 20:11.)

We are all Ben-hadads. We, too, swell and boast and shake our fists and strut our shortsighted way in our brief time, wagging our wise heads in blind self-approval, clasping time and space to our bosoms as though these were all there are, as though our now were forever—boasting too, even to the very King of Israel, "Thy silver and thy gold are mine!" Even worse we crow, "Thy children, too, are mine!" as though our fellow men were ours to use and the things we have on earth *were* ours—which they are not.

The things of the earth are ours only to use to prove ourselves by. But we are promised that they may become ours, if we prove worthy in the fight.

But mostly, we don't bother. We hear about the struggle and perhaps think about it; we may even talk about it, but we neglect to practice it. We stand foolishly gaping on the fringe of the battle, occasionally boasting some victory and sometimes even claiming some of the victor's spoils. But we never really enter the battle. We spend our lives in preludes, forgetting that our mortal day must pass and the evening come when each of us will cease to gird his harness, when each must tell his actuality—what his great moments were amid the fray; what he has learned about loving others and himself.

What then shall we say of spoils and the rewards of battle?

Rewards, such as Israel's King can give, can never come to those who talk only of battle yet shun the fight, who talk of insights and repentance but never change. It's not enough to spend our lives intending to succeed, intending to participate, girding always to the battle, fooling ourselves that our good intentions *are* the battle, and that by our much intendings we've surely done our part and secured our victory.

All earthly beginnings come to an end. And when evening arrives, and the time for valor in this mortal fray is past, and each of us stands in the image he has made of himself, to make his claim for his reward, what then? We cannot then set aside the requirements. The King of Israel, even Jesus Christ, has set them firm: "They who keep their first estate shall be added upon; and they who keep not their first estate shall not have glory in the same kingdom with those who keep their first estate; and they who keep their second estate shall have glory added upon their heads for ever and ever." (Abraham 3:26.)

God help me, and you, and all of us to meet this great reward, to remember always who we are and who others are, and to truly love those who come to us for love, in this world and out of it. There is more day to dawn than we perceive. Mortality is but a moment. God grant us eyes to see, ears to hear, and hearts to feel, that we may know our lives as they really are, bright white dawnings of great expectations, our souls' sunrise toward a shining noonday fullness of both body and spirit, a fullness of being, earned, achieved, maintained, and enjoyed with those we love, forever and ever.

Index

primary love is love for, 50; develop patterns of action matching, 55; as source of love supplies, 144-45; thrives on truth, 145; prayer to identify, 146

Spiritual point of view, 31-39

Spirituality, achieving, 125

Stress, handled by escape, 71-72

Styles: are patterns of behavior, 55-56; are defense systems, 62; of substitute self, 63-69; therapy can become substitute, 68; detected in way stress handled, 70; psychosis, 71-72; schizophrenia, 72-74; neurosis, 74-77; psychosomatic, 77-78; personality disorder, 79-81; transient situational personality disorder, 81-82; are disorders, 83; in female inadequacy, 117-18; in male inadequacy, 118-19

Substitute self: misleading voice of, 33; discovering styles of, 63-69; styles of, are tools of devil, 71

Sufficiency motivations, 93

"Supermother," 118

Symbiotic relationships, 40-41

Symptoms: are surface, 63; discerning, to gain control, 95; examples of, 95-96

Targets: right, 40-52; primary and secondary, 47; must be external, 25-26

Thoreau, Henry David, 9, 130

Thoughts: precede deeds, 149; need to be sensitive to, 149-50; steps in controlling, 150-52

Time consciousness, 99-100

Transferences, 104-5

Transient situational personality disorder, 81-82

True love is always giving, 50-51

Tuning people out, 43

Understanding: crucial to repentance, 57; yields love, 126-27

Uniqueness, 128-29

Unisexuality, 111

Vocational dominance, 118

Voice: tone in communication, 14; of spirit speaks first, 28; of world self, 28-29

Woman: weighed 247 lbs., 25-26; washed hands frequently, 75-76

Word association game, 12

Words, in communication, 14

Wordsworth, William, 2

World self, 25, 28, 31-32, 35

Worth, built into spirit, 16

Wrong things for wrong reasons, 86-87

Young, Brigham, 19, 53, 143